MW00872639

A WHOLE LOT OF
SHENANIGANS

All the Best
Charlie McMahon

BY
CHARLIE A. MCMAHON

Copyright © 2018 Charlie A. McMahon

All rights reserved.

ISBN-10: 1722823267
ISBN-13: 978-1722823269

Editors
Jennifer McMahon
Krissy Heather

Cover & Graphics
Kristina Ackerman

Cover Concept & Foreword
Benji Kurtz

A WHOLE LOT OF SHENANIGANS

DEDICATION

This book is dedicated to all of the people out there that work or have worked in retail, food service, hospitality, and with the public in general.

You've witnessed and dealt with stupidity, arrogance, brashness, disrespect, and rudeness to a degree that nobody outside of your line of work could ever understand.

Stay strong, lean on each other and hopefully one day you'll look back on it all and laugh. I sure did.

Keep the Faith,
Charlie McMahon

"Welcome to the working week
Oh, I know it don't thrill you, I hope it don't kill you
Welcome to the working week
You gotta do it till you're through it, so you better get to it"
-Elvis Costello
"Welcome to the Working Week"
1977 Stiff Records

A WHOLE LOT OF SHENANIGANS

FOREWORD

"I'll tell you what I shoulda said!" "You know what I should've done to that guy?" If you're like me, you've reflected on some unbelievable statement or action by some shady member of the general public (that clearly neither you nor I are part of) and thought to yourself – if only I said what I *really* thought – or had dreamt up the perfect revenge and executed it exactly as intended...but alas – so many creative ideas, but, you know....life.

Well, I'm here to tell you, the guy who actually comes up with the clever retort and sticks the proverbial (or perhaps literal) banana in the tailpipe – he does, in fact, exist, and you happen to have been fortunate enough to have picked up a copy of his book.

Although my wife and I have been friends with Charlie and his wife Jen for only a couple of years, there was a connection that felt as though we had known each other for many years. Perhaps it's our shared affinity for music of the 70s and 80s. Maybe it's the New York roots of the McMahons, and my lineage in the northeast (though I was born and raised in the south). Whatever the reason, there is never a visit or text message exchange that doesn't include a good laugh and a hearty dose of sarcasm. When Charlie's in a room (or even just a conversation), smiles will ensue – guaranteed.

Charlie seems to have found time to live several lifetimes' worth of jobs, pranks and memories. Even today, it's not unusual for Charlie to tell us a story from a career we didn't even know had happened. "Oh yeah, you know, when I managed that spoon museum…" or "…have I not told you that I collected tolls on the Tappan-Zee for a few years?" I'm not really sure how the math works that he is only as old as he is and has lived all these experiences, but I've decided to suspend my disbelief at this point.

Although this book contains anecdotes only from Charlie's most-recent career managing a parking lot, his library of stories is deep. As a musicologist, he might say that he's got stories that are not only hits, but plenty of 'album cuts' as well. Make sure to tell a friend about this book – we have to convince him to write the next one. Trust me, there are several books' worth of life to get on paper.

Enough from me. Turn the page, strap yourself in, and enjoy living vicariously through Charlie McMahon. If you're from the south, the language may make you clutch your pearls once or twice, but bless his heart, Charlie's a yankee. They talk different up there. Pour yourself a tall glass of iced tea (sweet if you're here in the south), but don't drink more than a sip at a time – you don't want to spray it all over yourself.

Benji Kurtz

INTRODUCTION

Well, How Did I Get Here?

I grew up in a middle class household. Both of my parents worked in the supermarket business. Back then, my parents were able to be a part of the middle class on their supermarket salaries. They also had pension benefits, which gave them some financial security once they retired. My Dad and Mom worked for the same supermarket chain, and in the same store, for many years. My Dad was with the company for over thirty years and my Mom for close to twenty. They retired with pensions and a boatload of crazy retail stories.

My parents' jobs were physically demanding. My Dad worked in the dairy department unloading trucks, stocking shelves, keeping things neat and organized, taking inventory, and helping customers. My Mom was on the front lines as a cashier for many years before being promoted into the floral department. The job definitely took a physical toll on both of them, especially as they got older. But the mental toll from dealing with the public seemed to affect them even more. My Dad rarely complained about work. Occasionally, he'd tell a story about a run in with a crazy customer, but, for the most part, he went in day after day for 30 years without complaining. My Mom, on the other hand, was always very vocal about her job. She would come home with unbelievable stories about what customers said and did. My Mom exaggerates a lot, so we always took what she said with a grain of salt. We figured these stories probably happened but not to the extent she described. At sixteen years old, I got a job in retail and realized that my mom was not always exaggerating when it came to work stories.

My first "real" job, other than paper routes, mowing lawns, and side hustles, was at Herman's World of Sporting Goods at a mall on Long Island, New York. I started in September 1987, just as my Junior year of high school got underway. I worked in the athletic shoe department selling sneakers, sports cleats, golf shoes, ice skates, rollerblades, and other athletic footwear. The job was pretty simple: get sneakers and shoes out of the stockroom in the size and model the customers requested. Some customers were difficult, but back then I was young and naïve and thought only the best of people, so it did not get to me all that much.   Over the next two years, I was promoted into management. With each promotion came more shenanigans and more craziness from the public.

I moved on to several other retail companies as an assistant manager and then store manager, managing hundreds of people and millions of dollars in sales before finally putting an end to my retail career in 1998. After almost eleven years, I had my fair share of people crapping in fitting rooms, trying to sleep overnight on patio furniture displays, fighting over 25 cent coupons, and bludgeoning each other on Black Friday. There had to be a better way! I spent the next 10 years in the corporate world at IT and pharmaceutical companies as a buyer, a purchasing manager, and as a logistics manager.

After over 20 years, I was burned out with the public, office politics, and working my ass off to make other people money. I decided to pursue my passion and start my own DJ company. Weddings and events were big business in New York, so there was money to be made. It took a little while, but my business really started to grow, and, before long, I was booked every weekend. It was refreshing dealing with people that were happy and excited about their upcoming events.

After a couple of years building the DJ business in New York, my wife and I decided to relocate to the suburbs of Atlanta, Georgia. My wife had a job she could easily transfer and I would start the DJ business back up in Atlanta. I was always one of those proud, die hard New Yorkers, but, after seeing friends who left New York improve their quality of life, I was convinced that there had to be something to it. We took the leap and moved to the Peach State.

After about a year in Georgia working on the DJ business, I took a Monday through Friday job at a real estate office doing marketing for an agent we knew. I kept DJing on the weekends. The woman who ran the real estate team turned her office into an old-fashioned soap opera, with lots of drama and backstabbing. I left after telling her how I really felt about her and the situation. I did not show any southern hospitality.

In fall 2015, I started driving for Uber to supplement the DJ business. I met people from all walks of life, heard some crazy stories, and made some decent money. When Uber cut the rate for drivers and I considered gas prices, maintenance, and wear and tear on my vehicle, I decided it did not make financial sense to keep driving for Uber. I closed out 2015 by DJing a few holiday parties and welcomed in 2016!

In January 2016, I decided it was finally time to write the book about my crazy family and childhood that I wanted to write for as long as I can remember. I have compiled notes and outlines for the book for a couple of decades. On Monday, January 11, 2016, I finally sat down to get started. About four hours and 10 pages in, my phone rang. It was a friend, so I answered. My friend said that I was on speaker phone and he was there with his boss, who had a side business as the co-owner of a parking lot. His boss and his boss' wife, the parking lot co-owners, were looking for someone to work at their parking lot. They asked if I was interested in the job. I said I would definitely like to know more and we set up a meeting later that day for me to meet the wife and discuss the job.

When I arrived at the parking lot, I was greeted by the wife who invited me inside the tiny payment shack. We discussed the job, salary, hours, and the fact that she and her husband had just fired their son from being the parking attendant because he was unreliable and making mistakes. Her main concern was hiring someone who was reliable. I told her she found the right guy. She told me I'd be starting on Monday, January 25 at 7:30am. I knew I was overqualified for this job, but it would give me something to do during the week when there were no DJ events. Unfortunately, my book writing would have to wait.

My first day at the parking lot was brutally cold, and not just by Atlanta standards, with temperatures in the teens. I arrived at 7:20 am and waited for the owner to arrive to open up the shack. When the owner arrived, we started the business day, and I jumped right in. She seemed impressed that I caught on so quickly, but I explained that I had worked retail for eleven years. I noticed several things that immediately that seemed off, including poor and confusing signage around the parking lot and no controls to prevent people from walking off without paying.

But, I was not the owner, and this was my first day, so I did not say anything. Not yet, anyway.

About a month after I started, the business became 100 percent my responsibility. I made repairs, printed detailed signage, and got things up to par as best I could. I only saw the owners at the end of each work day when one of them would arrive with a bag to take the day's money that I had driven myself crazy amassing. Business at the parking lot went up twenty-five percent my first year, and I was working overtime at the lot on nights and weekends for festivals and events while still trying to juggle my DJ business. Between the long hours, lack of time off, and the daily shenanigans at the parking lot, I was quickly getting burned out.

Despite my exhaustion, I was pleasant to everybody that arrived at the parking lot, and I understood that many were going through matters in court, whether their fault or not, that put them in a foul mood. I knew it was a place that not many people wanted to be; so, I went out of my way to be personable, even when I was not feeling it. Everyone got the benefit of the doubt until they were blatantly rude, disrespectful, or just plain stupid. Then they got what was coming to them. For the first time in my working life, I was able to give it right back to those who deserved it and had to answer to nobody. It was the most liberating feeling -- Imagine being able to tell someone that deserved it to "fuck off" or being able to call someone out for acting like a fool without any repercussions. Not having to take shit from people was like having a ton of bricks lifted off my back. The look on the faces of those who thought they were going to get away with being rude and obnoxious was priceless. They did not expect a friendly, otherwise nice guy to turn on a dime and give it back tenfold. Toss in my New York accent, which stands out like a sore thumb here in the South, and it truly made a comedy for the ages.

Although I often say "I hate people," that is not really accurate. I like people, I am just contemptuous of total, complete, stupidity. Unfortunately, I was exposed to an inordinate degree of stupidity at that parking lot. After two years of documenting my encounters with hundreds of rude and stupid people, I decided to write a book of short stories to share with the world. I do have to thank my friends who encouraged me to write this book after reading my daily stories on social media. So here they are, the stories from a courthouse parking lot managed by a no nonsense New Yorker in a suburban Georgia town. The names of the characters in the book have been changed to protect the innocent...or guilty. You decide.

Digging for Dollars

You would be hard pressed to find a better feeling than those first few warm days after a long, cold winter. Here in the South, the warmth comes on suddenly, unlike in New York where spring and those warmer temperatures took their sweet time to arrive. But regardless of how long it takes to heat up, warmer temperatures are always welcome. Along with warmer temperatures come the sights and sounds of spring and summer: that first ring of the ice cream truck's bell; a song that immediately makes you think of summer; children playing outside; birds singing in the trees; people riding around with car windows down; the first barbeque of the season; planting flowers in your flower beds and planters; and the smell of fresh cut grass. With the onset of the spring season comes new beginnings, spring cleaning, and the "out with the old and in with the new" mentality. A rebirth of spirit, if you will.

In the parking lot, the first warm days of the year took on a much different meaning. There were no birds singing, no ice cream truck, no pretty flowers to admire. Nothing would make you aware it was warming up except for one thing: titty money. The first warm days in the parking lot were the official start of titty money season. Titty money season is a six or seven-month period that starts in April and winds down in late September or October, depending on when temperatures cool down and titties are tucked away until the following spring.

Titty money season starts in a flash, a literal flash. When you least expect it, a 54F breast will make its way into your field of vision as the owner of that 54F breast digs into a sweaty crevice to retrieve her cash or debit card. You see, titty money is rarely tendered by a woman with perky breasts. You have a better chance of getting struck by lightning twice than witnessing a woman with an average or voluptuous chest reaching in her bra for cash or a credit card. Being on the receiving end of titty money is not what I envisioned. In my perfect world, a well-endowed woman with perky breasts would approach the payment booth, make eye contact, slowly reach in her blouse to retrieve her payment method, perhaps lick her lips, whip her hair back into the soft spring breeze as she hands you a cool, crisp five-dollar bill which faintly smells like her perfume or body spray.

Yeah, that is not how it happens in the lot. The reality is that a sloppy woman with large sweaty, breasts approaches the payment booth. When I ask her if she is paying with cash or a card, she will tell me how she's paying and then proceed to reach into her bra and start digging. With my vantage point from the window being about a foot or two above the customers', sort of like a judge's view, I pretty much see everything. Things that unfortunately cannot be unseen. As the digging continues, no shame is felt by the titty money tenderer. As the other people in line and I are watching, she will openly search, going from left titty to right titty, over, under, side to side until the payment method is located, somewhere near her knees. The titty money tenderer then hands me a very warm, moist bill or a very warm and slippery debit or credit card. My look of disgust usually says it all, so much so that I have had a few titty money tenderers ask me what was wrong. "Oh nothing" I would say as I was pumping a quart of hand sanitizer into my hands while calculating in my head how many more months were left until the end of titty money season and praying that there would be no Indian Summer.

The only form of payment that is as bad, or perhaps worse than titty money, is sock or shoe money. Sock and shoe money unfortunately wasn't limited to the warm months; this was a year-round method of payment. I will admit, back in the early 80s, when I was ten years old or so, I used to place money in the bottom of my sneakers. I did this for a couple of reasons, first, I was TEN years old. Second, at the time, most of the kids, including me, wore skin tight athletic shorts. You know, the ones with the elastic waistband and the colored stripe going down the side of the shorts that continued around the leg opening? Those shorts had NO POCKETS. I needed a place for my candy or baseball card money while I was out playing just in case I ended up down at the corner gas station or deli.

So, to watch grown ass men, dressed for court, taking their dress shoes off and looking for money in their shoes, or even worse, in their socks, is absolutely dumbfounding. They clearly have pockets in their pants, a pocket on their shirt, and in many cases a pocket or two in their suit jackets. On many occasions, I downright refused the foot sweat soaked, toe cheese ridden bills. This led to some verbal altercations, in which I was a willing participant. I would rather deal with a minute or two of mixing it up with someone I called a filthy fucker, than smell their soaked, smelly, toe jam ridden ten-dollar bill aroma from the cash drawer all day long.

Then of course there was the change scraper method of payment: under the car mat, under the car seat, and wherever else they could scrape up a coin. These change scrapers were always great to deal with during the morning rush when a line of people were waiting to pay, along with the titty money tenderers and sock or shoe money men, whose bills were marinating in the morning heat. The change scrapers show up at the window and throw down a pile of uncounted pennies, dimes, nickels and quarters for me to count, complete with pet hair, a couple of McDonald's French fries dating back to the grunge era, a few coins fused together by some sticky substance I would rather not think about, foreign coins, and green pennies that were moldy from extra condensation in the change scraper's 1987 Plymouth with a garbage bag used as a window.

Wallets were invented in the late 1600s, shortly after the introduction of paper currency to western civilization. Change purses came well before that. The first purse dates back to somewhere around 3,300 BC. The oldest known purse was found on Otzi the iceman who lived somewhere between 3400 and 3100 BC. Even Otzi did not store shit in his shoes, and I am quite certain Otzi's wife wasn't digging in between her titties for items of value. She was too classy, and honestly, the risk of frostbite was too high. Only people in the parking lot could make people from the Copper Age look modern and sophisticated.

Animal House

I've had pets for as long as I can remember. Growing up, our family had four dogs who we loved and considered part of our family. As of this writing, I have three dogs and a cat. Two of our beloved dogs have passed in recent years, after long and wonderful lives. Over the past decade or two, I've noticed that many people, including myself, treat our pets more like children than we do like animals. I think that is a welcome change, especially when those pets have been rescued from a shelter and given a second chance at a long life, filled with love.

With pets, just like with children, come major sacrifices. I learned quickly about those sacrifices when I rescued my first dog back in my bachelor days. There were many parties, events, after work happy hours, weekends away and various other things I declined because I knew Bruce, my dog, was waiting at home for me. When I knew a work day would be particularly long, I made arrangements with neighbors, friends or a pet sitter to look in on Bruce to be sure he went outside, had a treat or two, and got some daytime attention. Life happens and sometimes you have to be at work or somewhere for an extended period of time. But, pet owners have a responsibility to their pets and should make the appropriate arrangements for them in advance. Unfortunately, that was not always the case at the parking lot.

Mornings at the lot were crazy, to say the least. On an average morning, I had 80 to 110 cars arriving within a 30 to 45-minute span. I had to process payments, answer questions, direct people to the correct courthouse, ensure people were not running off without paying, correct people's parking when they were out of the lines, and a host of other mundane tasks. Doing it all alone was pure hell. On one particular busy morning, as I was assisting a line of customers, I saw a young couple walking towards me at the payment booth with what looked like two pet cages. I processed the line of customers and then the couple stepped up to the window. I could no longer see whatever I thought I saw them holding, because at the window, I could only see them from the waist up. So perhaps I imagined it.

ME: Good morning, will you be using cash or card to pay for your parking this morning?

FEMALE PET PEDDLER: Can you watch Cindy and Corky while we are in court?

ME: Who are Cindy and Corky?

FEMALE PET PEDDLER: They are our ferrets.

She proudly hoisted the ferret cages in the air like she had just won the Stanley Cup as Cindy and Corky, one white, and one brown, ran around inside the cages.

ME: Ummm….that would be a big no.

MALE PET PEDDLER: Excuse me? Aren't you an animal lover?

ME: Yes, I am, but you do realize where you are, right? This is a parking lot, not an animal daycare or boarding center.

FEMALE PET PEDDLER: It is sooooo cold out and we don't want to leave Cindy and Corky in the car! You have heat in there, right?

ME: I have to ask, why are you bringing ferrets to court?

FEMALE PET PEDDLER: Looooong story, but really, you can't just watch them for a few hours? They already ate, you don't have to feed them. Just keep them company, and warm!

ME: I am sorry, as tempting as your offer is, I cannot watch or take responsibility for your pets. This is a parking lot. One of you will have to stay in the car with Cindy and Corky with the heat running or you will have to take them home or to an appropriate animal daycare center.

The couple walked away angry with me and truly stunned that I had the audacity to refuse to spend the day with their precious Cindy and Corky. How did they know I was not some sicko with a ferret fetish? I could have been a closeted ferret fucker for all they knew. Or perhaps I was running a ferret fighting ring right there in the booth where people could come to the window and place their money on Cindy or Corky. For the record, I think Cindy would have taken Corky in two rounds, but we will never know. I found it completely insane that someone would not only bring ferrets to court but be willing to trust a complete stranger with their pets.

After the ferret fracas, I wondered exactly how the pet peddlers' pre-court pet sitting conversation went that morning. I imagine it went something like this:

MALE PET PEDDLER: What are we going to do with Cindy and Corky today while we are in court?

FEMALE PET PEDDLER: Hmmm, great question honey! I hadn't given it much thought.

MALE PET PEDDLER: How about we leave them with your mom?

FEMALE PET PEDDLER: No, she's working the morning shift at Wal-Mart.

MALE PET PEDDLER: Can't we just leave them home in their cages?

FEMALE PET PEDDLER: No honey, looong story, but we just can't. I have an idea! How about we drop them off with the guy who works at the parking lot outside the courthouse?! He must be an animal lover and he'll just fall in love with Cindy and Corky. I mean who wouldn't?! Just look at them!

MALE PET PEDDLER: I have to say, you come up with some great ideas! Oh shit, look at the time, we are going to be late, let's load Cindy and Corky in the car and head to court! Let's just hope the parking lot guy isn't a ferret fucker, like the guy in that video we watched the other night.

FEMALE PET PEDDLER: That was a squirrel honey, not a ferret.

MALE PET PEDDLER: Could have sworn it was a ferret. Anyway, we better get going. I guess the parking lot guy will have to do.

For the record, Cindy and Corky were left in the car for the couple of hours the pet peddling couple were in court. The mammals were granted access to roam around inside the vehicle and were last seen sunbathing on the dashboard of their Toyota Camry. To the best of my knowledge, no ferret wagers were placed on ferrets fighting and no ferrets were harmed or molested that day.

Gimme' A Break!

No 1980s childhood was complete without the watching of television sitcoms. Back then, I knew what nights the shows I loved were on and I was ready and in front of the television set when they started. In most cases I acted as the remote myself, getting up and down to change the channel. Before we had a VCR, if I missed my show, I was out of luck. So many television sitcom icons came from the 1980s. Michael J. Foxx as Alex P. Keaton on Family Ties, Emmanuel Lewis as Webster, Gary Coleman as Arnold on Diff'rent Strokes, Kirk Cameron as Mike Seaver on Growing Pains, Robert Guillaume as Benson, and Nell Carter as Nell Harper on Gimme' A Break are just a few.

Gimme' A Break was on television for 6 seasons or so. Nell Carter, the star of the show, was also pretty well known for her performances on Broadway. She even won a Tony Award for "Ain't Misbehavin" in the late 1970s. Nell also was nominated for a couple of Emmys and Golden Globes for her role in Gimme' A Break. She was also a regular panelist on the popular game show, "Match Game." So, during the 1980s, Nell Carter was a prominent name on television and Gimme' A Break was a popular show. My siblings and I loved Gimme' A Break.

Fast forward a few decades. First, some background: each morning I coned off two parking spaces located on either side of my booth. I wanted to avoid people idling in the spots, filling up the booth with emissions. I also did this so that if the lot was full, a couple of my regular customers would have a place to park. Call it V.I.P. service for the regulars.

On one warm and sunny morning, a woman came up to pay for her vehicle that she had just parked. After paying for her vehicle and heading off to court, she turned around and came back to the booth with a "very important question."

OBLIVIOUS OLIVIA: Could I give you an extra five dollars for my friend? She is on her way over here and has no money or credit card with her.

ME: Ma'am I would love to, but there's no guarantee I'll have spaces available when she arrives, so I don't want to take your money if I can't ensure she'll have a spot.

OBLIVIOUS OLIVIA: Can she park in that space? Could you please hold it for her? *Pointing to one of the spaces with an orange traffic cone in it.*

ME: Ok, sure. What is her name, so I will know who she is when she arrives? Please tell her to come up and give me her name so I can take the cone away for her.

OBLIVIOUS OLIVIA: Ok, great, thanks so much! Her name is Nell Carter.

ME: Oh, gimme a break!

I assumed this was an obvious reference to the television show.

OBLIVIOUS OLIVIA: What do you mean, give you a break? Are you going to help me out or not? If you can't do it just say so! Why are you being difficult?

ME: Ma'am I was referencing the TV show, "Gimme' A Break," where Nell Carter was the star of the show! She has the same name as your friend.

OBLIVIOUS OLIVIA: Never heard of it!

ME: *Now completely puzzled.* Ummm, ok I'll save the spot for Nell.

As the woman walked towards court, I was left wondering a couple of things: 1) How has an African American woman in her mid-fifties never heard of Nell Carter or Gimme' A Break? I'm a white guy from the suburbs of Long Island in my mid-forties and I watched Gimme' A Break and I know who Nell Carter is; and 2) How do you have a friend who shares a name with a celebrity and somehow that has never come up in conversation? If I were friends with a Tony Danza or a Ricky Schroder, I'd be relentless with "Who's the Boss" and "Silver Spoons" jokes and references. But, the story does not end with Oblivious Olivia not knowing Nell Carter (the celebrity).

A few minutes later a young lady, talking on a cell phone, pulled up in front of my booth and started pointing at the coned off space reserved for Nell. Could this be Nell Carter?

ME: *Shouting out of the booth.* Ma'am, can I help you!?

YOUNG LADY: *Shouting out of her car window.* Can I have that spot, there are no other spaces left!?

ME: Sorry ma'am, that spot is reserved for Nell Carter!

YOUNG LADY: Nell Carter?! Nell Carter is coming here?

ME: Indeed, she is. As a matter of fact, Nell's friend just paid and reserved that very spot for her!

YOUNG LADY: Oh my God! That's unbelievable, thanks anyway!

YOUNG LADY: *Speaking into her phone.* You're never going to believe this; Nell Carter is coming here today! They reserved a spot for her! She's on her way! .... Yeah, the Gimme' A Break lady!

Actually, no. "Gimme' A Break" lady, Nell Carter, died a decade and a half ago on January 23, 2003, and is buried in Los Angeles. A much livelier Nell Carter showed up about 15 minutes later and claimed her reserved parking space with no fanfare, requests for autographs, paparazzi harassment or attention of any sort. Fake Nell went on to be the closest thing I would ever have to a celebrity encounter in the more than two years I worked at the parking lot.

I Declare Stupidity!

During my first year working at the parking lot, customers were able to pay for parking a couple of different ways. If they were paying cash, they would come up to the window of my shack and pay the parking fee in exchange for a ticket that they would place on their dashboard. I did not have a credit card reader, so if they were using a credit or debit card, they were forced to use a kiosk that was located right outside the shack window.

The kiosk has on screen instructions, instructions printed on the machine just above the screen, and a giant instructional sign taped to it that I posted. Despite that, I would say more than seventy percent of customers still could not figure out how to work the kiosk. I would shout, step by step, verbal instructions to almost every customer using the kiosk. This exchange turned what should have been a 15 to 20 second transaction into several minutes. This, in turn, would make the other customers waiting in line even more angry. At the parking lot, during the week when most people were headed to court, they were already pissed off that they had to be there, stressed, and usually running late. By Wednesday each week, after giving verbal instructions to hundreds of customers using the kiosk, I had no voice left.

I mentioned this problem to the owners multiple times, and suggested that a credit/debit card terminal I could use at the window would eliminate confusion, speed up the line at peak times, and save my voice. My suggestion fell on deaf ears for almost a year. Finally, after several of my intense rants to the owners, they caved in and got a credit card terminal that I could use inside the shack.

The customers felt the difference immediately. I posted a large sign on the outside payment kiosk to cover up the display screen and card slot that said "Please Pay At Window." I could now process payments by card in under fifteen seconds without a giving a verbal instruction manual for every transaction. The customers loved the change too, because it got them on their way in a flash. And the new payment terminal let me accept Apple Pay and Samsung Pay that the younger people were using. What a great time to be alive and working in a parking lot!

But, as with anything, came stupid people. One morning I was once again mired in the morning rush. As I was processing customer after customer, I noticed a guy yapping away on his cell phone while fucking around with the kiosk with the huge "PAY AT WINDOW" sign I had plastered on it. By the time I got everyone in line processed and on their way, which was all of about five minutes, the assclown was off his phone, hostile, and ready to start a ruckus.

ATM ASSCLOWN: This is some motherfuckin' bullshit!

ME: What is wrong sir?

ATM ASSCLOWN: *Showing me the FIVE 5 dollar receipts for parking space twelve that he had just paid for.* My money didn't come out!

ME: What money?

ATM ASSCLOWN: The money out of your ATM, see! *Handing me his five receipts.* I should have gotten 25 dollars out, here are my five 5 dollar withdrawal receipts. You must be out of motherfuckin' cash!

ME: Sir, that's not an ATM, that's a parking payment kiosk. You weren't taking cash out, you just paid for parking spot number twelve, five times. These are your parking payment receipts.

ATM ASSCLOWN: How was I supposed to know that shit? That's some deceitful bullshit right there!

ME: Sir, there's a big sign on the kiosk that says "PAY AT WINDOW" and there are also instructions on it explaining what the kiosk is for.

ATM ASSCLOWN: It looks just like an ATM! That's some bullshit right there!

ME: Sir, when has an ATM ever asked you for a parking space number to get started? It is clearly a parking payment kiosk.

ATM ASSCLOWN: RIDICULOUS! Can I have a motherfuckin' refund? I'm late, I have no time for this bullshit, I gotta be in court in fifteen minutes!

ME: Sir, I cannot process refunds. Your best bet would be to call your bank, tell them what happened, and dispute the transaction. Just declare stupidity.

ATM ASSCLOWN: Oh, just call the bank?

ME: Yes, sir.

ATM ASSCLOWN: And declare what?

ME: Stupidity.

ATM ASSCLOWN: Ok. Can I call now so you're here just in case they want to talk to you? I gotta get this off my mind before I go into court and forget!

ME: Sure, sir.

ATM Assclown dialed the bank with his cell phone set on speaker phone. He went through a myriad of automated menus until he finally got a live customer service representative on the line.

BANK REP: Thank you for calling Wells Fargo, can I help you?

ATM ASSCLOWN: Yes, I need to declare stupidity.

BANK REP: Excuse me sir, what is it that you need assistance with?

ATM ASSCLOWN: I was told that I need to declare stupidity so I can get my 25 dollars back. Can you help me?

BANK REP: Sir, I still am not sure what I can assist you with. You need 25 dollars back? Did someone use your card without your permission? Shall I connect you to our fraud division?

ATM ASSCLOWN: No! The parking machine stole my money, I thought it was an ATM. The guy here told me to call you to declare stupidity so I can get my money back. I'm declaring stupidity for my refund! Can you help me?

BANK REP: *Talking through laughter.* Ok sir, let me see what I can do for you today. We'll try to get this resolved for you.

After about five minutes spent on the phone declaring his stupidity, ATM Assclown got it all worked out and went on with his day. As I watched ATM Assclown saunter out of sight, I was certain that he would be declaring stupidity sometime again in the very near future, most likely in front of a judge.

An Apple a Day

As I get older, I find it becomes more difficult to keep up with the latest technology. As soon as I figure out the latest and greatest technology, something else comes along to take its place. Just a few months ago, I upgraded my music library from 8-tracks to these much more efficient, cassette tapes. They take a while to fast forward and rewind (with or without a pencil) to the song you want to hear, but so worth the wait! Crystal clear sound! But now I hear that there are these shiny discs that have music on them, CDs I think they're called. I will have to check those out. I just cannot keep up with all this advancing technology.

It did not take long for me to realize that technology was non-existent in the parking industry. I started working at the parking lot in January 2016, and it turned out that the owners had just discovered credit card technology about a month or two earlier. To them, accepting a credit card as a form of payment was cutting edge! The parking lot I worked in was now in 1975, while the two adjacent parking lots were still in the 1950s, only taking cash. We were pioneers! I was shocked that the owners had jumped so far ahead, to an "advanced" electronic kiosk for cutting edge credit card payments, rather than easing their way in by implementing the carbon paper copy first. The IT and business strategy at the parking lot seemed to be, wait thirty years until the technology has been proven, then go for it.

The outside kiosk, although new to the owners, was already outdated the day it was installed. It had no touch screen, had a 1970s interface, only took exact change if paying with cash, and was far from user friendly since it frustrated just about every customer that attempted to use it. But the owners thought it was the best thing since sliced bread was invented, right around the same time of that credit card kiosk.

As noted above, after a year of customer complaints, long lines to use the machine because it was so slow processing cards, long winded explanations to every customer on how to use it, and fifty or so of my rants to the owners, we got an additional, modern credit card terminal inside the booth, which enabled me to process payments quickly and efficiently.

With this new technology came new ways for the customers to pay for parking. Apple Pay and Samsung Pay were two of those new methods. I'll admit, I do not use Apple Pay with my iPhone, but I do know about the wallet app and how to set it up. I just do not want all my payment information stored on a device in case it gets lost, stolen or hacked. But, many people, including my wife, love the convenience. At the parking lot, Apple and Samsung Pay were a hit right away with the younger crowd, the lumberjack bearded hipsters, many of the attorneys, and the more tech savvy customers. From my perspective, on the other side of the window, it was fabulous! Not only lightning fast, but I did not have to handle credit cards that were in between titties, in socks, and in germ infested hands. I would simply hold up the small terminal and the customer could put their phone up to it and boom...done.

But, as you can probably guess by now, like with anything else, there had to be a person or two to gum up the works. One morning a young hipster looking gentleman approached the booth.

JOHNNY APPLESEED: OOOOOOOH, you take Apple Pay?

ME: Yes, sir, we do!

JOHNNY APPLESEED: Great, I'd like to pay with Apple Pay.

ME: Sure. Just let me know when you're set on your end and I'll cue up the transaction on the terminal.

JOHNNY APPLESEED: Oh, I'm ready.

ME: *Holding up the terminal to Johnny Appleseed's phone.* Sir, it didn't work, are you sure you had the application open and it was ready to transmit?

JOHNNY APPLESEED: Oh, I am sure. Let's try it again.

ME: Sure, Sir.

Now, the line was growing behind him, people were grumbling, and this cutting edge technology was taking an apple sized bite out of my ass.

ME: *Holding up the terminal once again and…. nothing.* Sir, something isn't right, this should take three seconds. Are you sure you have it set up correctly?

JOHNNY APPLESEED: Ummmm, yeah. I use it all the time.

ME: May I have a peek at your phone?

JOHNNY APPLESEED: Sure.

ME: *Realizing Johnny Appleseed was trying to pay me with a photo of his credit card from pictures on his camera roll.* Sir, this is just a photo of your credit card, you need to set up the wallet app in your phone with the credit card information in order to use Apple Pay. It's the application that sends a signal to the terminal, not just a picture.

JOHNNY APPLESEED: You do?

ME: Wait, I thought you used it all the time?

JOHNNY APPLESEED: *Now as red faced as an apple.* I must've been thinking of something else.

Johnny Appleseed, after backing up the line, not only had to endure the shame of paying with the outdated technology of an actual credit card, but had to turn around and face a dozen or so very amused people. Poor Johnny.

Later that afternoon an older lady, probably in her mid-70s, came up to pay and was very curious about paying via Apple.

ME: Good afternoon ma'am, can I help you?

LITTLE APPLE ANNIE: Yes, I was just reading your sign, what's this Apple Pay? People pay with apples? Why would you take apples? Do you give 'em to the poor? Don't they rot out in this heat or do you have air conditioning in there?

ME: *Holding in laughter.* No ma'am, Apple Pay is a way to pay with your phone. It refers to Apple the company, not the fruit.

LITTLE APPLE ANNIE: You got me there! I was gonna say, I ain't got no apples to give you, just good ol' green cash!

ME: No problem ma'am, we still accept that!

LITTLE APPLE ANNIE: *Handing me cash.* I'm glad. I don't know nothing about all these darn phones. Phone Shmone! My grandkids are always on those darn phones looking at Facingpage and Twatter and all those things. I tell them go outside and play, the Facingpage and Twatter will be there when you come in. So they go outside, and they bring the darn phones with 'em! I give up on those phones. I don't want any Facingpage or Twatter at my age! All they do is Twat and Facepage all day!

ME: *Laughing.* You are all set. Have a great day ma'am, hope to see you again. Be sure to bring your apples next time!

LITTLE APPLE ANNIE: *Laughing.* I will! Stay off that Twatter and Facingpage, they are evil!

As I drove home that afternoon, reflecting upon the day, I felt slightly younger and hip. At the very least, I knew what Apple Pay was. I knew not to bring a bushel of apples to a business that accepted Apple Pay and I also knew, unlike the hipster, that it involved more than just a photo of my credit card. Most importantly, I knew better than to say Twatter in public; it just did not seem right, especially in the current social climate. All that aside, with this never ending technology boom, what better time than now to upgrade to those CDs?

Liquid Gold

I have been fortunate to have had great friends over the years. Many I still keep in touch with via social media and some I have lost touch with because they are on social media rarely or not at all. Facebook is truly like a "This Is Your Life" episode when you look at your friends list. If you are on Facebook, and your friends list is anything like mine, it showcases friends from your school days, past jobs, people you met through other friends, and so on. Some are lifelong, close friends and some are more casual friends.

Some say the true meaning of friendship is not necessarily how often you see someone or how much time you spend with them, but rather knowing you can rely on each other through good times and bad (I just started humming "That's What Friends Are For" by Dionne & Friends). In all seriousness, true friends typically do things for each other that an acquaintance or a casual friend likely would not do. But, is there a limit to what you should expect or ask a friend to do? Are there also limits as to what to expect from a love interest, partner or spouse? Meat Loaf thought so when he wrote "I Would Do Anything for Love, But I Won't Do That." Twenty-five plus years later, and I still do not know what the hell he was talking about.

One hot summer day, I watched as a car pulled into a parking spot down at the far end of the parking lot. The car sat there for several minutes and then moved to an area along the perimeter of the parking lot, near the entrance, where I could not see it very well.

22

This has happened before. These were usually people who were waiting for someone to come out of court, and who did not want to pay for a parking spot. The owners did not allow this and expected me to lock up the booth each time this happened to investigate what the person was doing in the lot and kick them out if they were just waiting and did not want to pay. This almost always led to the person in the vehicle being confrontational, so I hated doing it. Typically, I would go out and investigate only if a vehicle was there for an extended period of time or if they were doing something egregious.

In this particular instance, I had given them about ten minutes, which would have been nine minutes too long for one of the owners, who, at more than sixty years old with a bum hip, would have shot out of the booth like Usain Bolt, fearing she might lose five dollars. As I approached the beat up, rust ridden jalopy, I saw two men in the front seats. The driver was sitting there talking on his phone. The passenger, however, had his seat reclined, with his pants unzipped, and was pissing into a bright yellow, antifreeze stained funnel that was attached to a pink water balloon. I was expecting an argument over a five-dollar parking fee. Instead I got an up close and personal view of a cock in a funnel attached to a water balloon. My great summer memories of childhood water balloon fights were now ruined forever.

DOPE DRIVER: *To the person on the phone*: I'mma have to call you back.

ME: Guys, I would ask what's going on, but I've already seen too much.

PISSING PETER: Man, I'm fillin' up dis balloon so my friend here can pass his drug test, aight?

23

It was apparent that Pissing Peter was going with the message in the Dionne & Friends song, as he did not think twice about pissing in that balloon for his pal. "For Good Times, and Bad Times, I'll Be On Your Side Forever More" seemed like Pissing Peter's mantra.

ME: Don't really need the explanation, just wanted to know what you were doing here for so long without paying.

DOPE DRIVER: We gonna leave, just waitin' on the balloon so I can go inside. He's gonna hop in the driver seat and drive it outta here when I go inside.

ME: Ok, guys. Have a good day. You seem to have things under control here.

PISSING PETER: *As he shook the last few drops of piss into the antifreeze stained funnel.* Don't say nuthin' man, please! My friend needs this or they gonna lock his ass up.

ME: Do you really think I am going to go around telling people I just saw a guy with his cock out, pissing into a water balloon in the parking lot!? How would that even come up in conversation?

DOPE DRIVER and PISSING PETER: *Laughing.* Thanks man! You ok!

Nah, I didn't tell anyone. I figured I would just include it in a book. I would have loved to hear the drug test result delivered by the probation officer. "Mr. Smith, your test came back clean for marijuana, cocaine and heroin, but you tested positive for Pennzoil and Prestone."

According to a court employee who I regularly spoke with at the parking lot, the art of pissing in a water balloon is quite common. He told me that he would find water balloons of urine stashed in the courthouse. He had found them in restrooms, behind sofa cushions, and in plants. Apparently, when the pisser or pissee feels that they might be under suspicion or if they are just paranoid, they'll ditch their liquid gold. So, if you are ever at or near a courthouse and happen to stumble upon a cock in a funnel attached to a water balloon, fear not, it is just a friend helping a friend. Because after all, that's what friends are for.

We All Need Somebody to Lean On

I bartended for a couple of years in the early 2000s. It was a fun job that allowed me to meet new and interesting people, and it brought in some extra cash to supplement my nine to five office gig. I bartended at a couple of different types of bars, one was a low key sports bar and the other was a very busy, always rowdy, pub. At the sports bar, especially on a slow night, folks came in to talk sports, music, and life. Yes, it is true what they say, a bartender is like a therapist for some. Some people just needed a place to go and to vent to a nonjudgmental stranger. Being a shoulder to lean on came with the territory, and you expected it. You would hear about marital problems, relationship issues, losing loved ones, and so forth.

At the courthouse parking lot, "Lean On Me" took on a whole different meaning. People from all different walks of life felt compelled to tell me, the parking lot attendant, all about their court cases and the problems in their lives which resulted in far too many moments when they gave me too much information, or TMI. After each one of these encounters, I would ask myself, what did I do to encourage this? Perhaps I should have greeted them with a simple "hello" rather than "hello, how are you today?" which may have opened up the door to this madness. Don't get me wrong, I am generally a pretty personable guy, but I do not exactly have a poker face. My facial expressions tell you exactly how I feel. Couldn't they see I was not even remotely interested in their stories? It did not matter. They made sure to give you a full briefing of their current situation, both legal and otherwise.

On one fun filled early afternoon, an older, disheveled woman approached the payment window.

ME: Good afternoon ma'am how are you today?

CRAIGSLIST CLAIRE: Oh, not too well. My dog is in the car, I had to bring him today. He has plenty of food and water and the windows are open, so tell those animal activist crazies not to break my goddamn windows!

ME: Ummmm...ok as long as he's taken care of I'm sure there won't be an issue, it's pretty cool out today.

CRAIGSLIST CLAIRE: Yeah, he's fine. I don't want those PETA nut jobs busting up my car. I see it on the news every day, people in other people's fucking business.

ME: I don't think you'll have a problem with PETA members here ma'am.

CRAIGSLIST CLAIRE: *No segue whatsoever.* Don't ever go on that Craigslist!

ME: Ummm, I wasn't really planning on it. I don't really have a need for Craigslist for anything.

CRAIGSLIST CLAIRE: Good, Craigslist is why I'm here. Goddamn roommate I found off that Craigslist! The fucking worst!

ME: Sorry you are having a problem with your roommate.

CRAIGSLIST CLAIRE: I can't get rid of this bitch, she eats all my fuckin' fried chicken! I came home from the senior center last night, and that bitch ate all my leftover fried chicken from KFC! Chicken.... all gone! Fuckin' bitch!

ME: Wow ma'am, I am sorry to hear that.

CRAIGSLIST CLAIRE: How do you just go and eat someone else's chicken without at least asking? What is the world coming to? Is nothing sacred?

ME: It's tough out there.

CRAIGSLIST CLAIRE: Oh, that's only the tip of the iceberg. The other morning, I was so constipated. I just couldn't go, you know, number two, so I figured the prune juice would help me. I went into the refrigerator, prune juice.... GONE! That bitch drank all my prune juice. Bitch has to go, bitch haaaaaaas to gooooooo! If I don't go number two regularly I'll get hemorrhoids. I don't need that! Bitch ain't giving me hemorrhoids!

ME: *Trying very hard not to laugh out loud.* I'm so sorry you are going through that ma'am.

CRAIGSLIST CLAIRE: I'm here to evict her. Going to tell the court about the chicken, the prune juice, not to mention my bananas and all the other snacks. If I don't go regularly I'll get hemorrhoids! I'll sue!

ME: I hope things work out for you.

CRAIGSLIST CLAIRE: Oh it will, I ain't gonna have it no more! Bitch is gone, so long bitch, ain't gonna have it no more! Eatin' my fuckin' chicken, no more!

Craigslist Claire walked off, as she continued to mumble about chicken, prune juice and hemorrhoids. I must have looked shell shocked because the next person in line, who heard the conversation, laughed and said "your face says it all!" Craigslist Claire came out of court about twenty minutes later waving what she claimed was a restraining order against her roommate. I am not sure if it instructed the roommate to keep away from Claire or her chicken. One can only guess in matters like these.

In addition to the one-time visitors like Craigslist Claire, there were also the repeat customers who gave constant updates on their court cases. Unfortunately, there was nowhere for me to hide in an 8' x 8' shack. I saw them approaching and it was like a tsunami rolling in, you knew it was coming, but there was nowhere to hide. You just had to ride it out.

One particular man came to court every month and stood at the window for thirty minutes at a time briefing me on his case, asking for advice, and rambling. According to him, he scammed his ex-girlfriend out of about fifteen thousand dollars. He openly admitted what he did but thought he had found legal loopholes around his misdeed. For the first year, he was representing himself and would Google laws and try to put his case together. He would then ask me, the parking lot attendant, for legal advice. I would encourage him to find a lawyer. "Do you know any good ones?" he'd ask. I'd always say no, because I did not want to expose any of the attorneys I was friends with or knew from working near the courthouse, to his insanity. He would stop any well-dressed person he saw walk by and ask them, "are you an attorney?" If they answered yes, he'd start telling them his scam story and most of them would either just end the conversation by giving him their business card or simply state that they were late for court to rid themselves of him. Occasionally, he would approach an attorney I knew relatively well and start asking about their legal services. When he'd turn his back on me to talk with them, I'd wave my hands and then shake my head "no" with a petrified expression on my face.

That particular guy was so full of shit. He forgot what he told me from visit to visit. One week he was a songwriter, the next, a Grammy award winner, Vietnam Veteran, real estate developer, investor, actor, financial planner...the list went on and on. He later admitted he lied to his current girlfriend, telling her he needed to borrow ten thousand dollars for a lucrative new business venture. She lent him the money and he drove around all day, shopping, eating out, and living high off of her cash infusion. One day, he told her he was going to a business meeting, for the fake business she invested in. As he filled me in on his latest scam, his cell phone rang and he said "oh shit, it's my girlfriend, watch this!" He answered the phone and told her "honey, I am just about to go into the business meeting, I'll call you when it is done." He hung up and said to me, "these bitches will believe anything!" He had no shame sharing all his shady dealings with me, as if I were impressed by it all. I left the job before his case concluded, but I am certain Judge Karma will get him sooner or later.

There were also those people who did something outrageous in the eyes of a civilized society, but perfectly fine in their eyes, so they wanted to share their stories with me too. The Ice Cream Cone Slapper comes to mind.

ME: Good morning ma'am, how are you today?

CONE SLAPPING SANDY: Terrible, it's bullshit that I have to be here!

ME: I'm sorry to hear that ma'am, I hope everything works out for you.

CONE SLAPPING SANDY: It better, I did nothing wrong! I can't believe I am even here.

ME: Well, best of luck in there.

CONE SLAPPING SANDY: Listen to this, please tell me what you think. I was at Wal-Mart shopping. This little toddler brat was running wild around the store with an ice cream cone. He ran right over my foot, right past me and rubbed chocolate ice cream all over my white pants! So, I ran after him and slapped the ice cream cone out of his hands. The police got called, and I was arrested for assault! I didn't hit the kid, I hit the ice cream cone! He should be charged with vandalism!

ME: You want a toddler with an ice cream cone charged with vandalism?

CONE SLAPPING SANDY: Well, his parents should be charged with it. You know what I mean. Do you think that was assault? What law says you can't hit an ice cream cone? His ice cream vandalized my pants! Again, never heard of a law that says you can't hit an ice cream cone, never heard of one, have you?

ME: I am not a lawyer ma'am; I just work in a parking lot. I'm sure all the ice cream cone statutes will be visited in court and it'll all be sorted out inside.

Cone Slapping Sandy went into court and about an hour later returned to the booth to tell me all about the latest developments in the cone slapping saga.

CONE SLAPPING SANDY: I am coming back in January, after the Christmas. Now I have to have this on my mind through the holidays. That little bastard ruined Christmas! Ruined Christmas with that fucking cone!

ME: Well, try to have a happy holiday.

CONE SLAPPING SANDY: I will have a Merry Christmas, not a Happy Holiday. We can say Merry Christmas again.

ME: I didn't know there was a time we couldn't say Merry Christmas, but ok. Take care now!

CONE SLAPPING SANDY: For eight years under that Obama, we couldn't say Merry Christmas! Now we can! This ain't a moooooslim country!

ME: Ok, whatever you say. Take Care.

CONE SLAPPING SANDY: Yeah, but before I go I need to ask you something.

ME: *Oh shit, here we go again.* Ok.

CONE SLAPPING SANDY: You seem like you have been working here a while. People must tell you about their cases. Do I have a case? Should I be worried? I hit the cone right, not the kid!

ME: I was not there ma'am, so I have no idea what you did. Also, I am not a lawyer, so I cannot give you any legal advice.

CONE SLAPPING SANDY: No, I am not asking for legal advice. I am asking you if someone ever told you about a case like this and what happened to them.

ME: You mean, about assaulting a child?

CONE SLAPPING SANDY: No, about slapping a cone! An ice cream cone. I never hit the kid, just the cone. Has anyone ever told you about hitting an object, like a cone?

ME: I have had many people tell me about their cases ma'am, but you are the first one to mention an assault on, or involving an ice cream cone, so I really can't offer you any story or outcome that would relate to yours.

CONE SLAPPING SANDY: *Seemingly surprised that ice cream cone assaults were not common.* Really, you never heard of something like this?

ME: Never in my life.

CONE SLAPPING SANDY: Oh well, just trying to put my mind at ease for Christmas with some information. This whole thing is going to kill me, I don't need this!

ME: Sorry I could not cite a legal precedent for you, Merry Christmas.

CONE SLAPPING SANDY: See, you said it! Ain't nothing wrong with sayin' Merry Christmas!

Cone Slapping Sandy exited the lot, hopeful she'd get her mind off the cone shenanigans for the holidays. I was so curious about ice cream cone laws that I went home that day and Googled "Ice Cream Cone Assaults" hoping to find a legal precedent to present to her in January, perhaps like Brown vs. Breyers, Plessy vs. Baskin Robbins, Miranda vs. Dairy Queen or even Gideon vs. Friendly's, but found nothing. Not even any legal opinions from Tom Carvel, Cookie Puss or Fudgie the Whale. There were however, several hundred cone slapping videos on YouTube, but all playful, none involving the assault of a cone licking toddler in Wal-Mart or elsewhere. Cone Slapping Sandy was in unchartered territory and would have to spend the holidays basking in 31 possible outcomes.

Cone Slapping Sandy came back to court in late January. When her day in court concluded, she informed me that she plead guilty to disorderly conduct and paid a fine, which ended her ice cream conundrum. For me, it was the beginning of yet another year of playing lawyer and therapist inside an 8' x 8' shack that kind of looked like a place you would buy an ice cream cone.

Run Forrest, Run!

Over the years, I've found that people will go to great lengths to avoid paying for things they really do not want to pay for. Some try to get illegal cable or borrow a friend or family member's Netflix credentials, others put off much needed auto body repair and use a bungee cord to keep their bumper in place, and others install that always attractive plastic bag window on their car to avoid getting a broken window fixed. Different people have different priorities. For some, driving around with red cellophane from last year's Easter basket flapping in the breeze as a substitute for their tail light while drinking a ten dollar Starbuck's Venti Frappuccino six days a week is perfectly acceptable. It all boils down to priorities.

Parking is something we all pretty much hate paying for, no matter what your priorities are, including yours truly. I've complained about 20, 30, even 40-dollar parking fees at concerts, stadiums, and various other venues I have been to over the years. Complained to the people I was with, that is. It never occurred to me to take it out on the parking attendant, or better yet, try to park my car but avoid paying altogether. I simply paid the fee, felt extremely violated immediately afterwards, but then took a long, hot shower when I got home and went on with my life.

At the parking lot, people would do anything and everything to either avoid paying or to let you know how unhappy they were about paying. Not a day went by without dozens of complaints lodged against the very concept of the parking fee. Most customers that were unhappy about the fee just mumbled as they reluctantly handed you their five dollars. Others gave a longwinded, impassioned speech in an attempt to get other parkers united in their anti-parking fee cause. The people who tried to avoid paying altogether were, by far, the most creative.

You might be wondering how someone could park without having to pay. They had this opportunity because unlike most parking lots and decks, the parking lot did not have one of those electronic arms that only allow entrance with a ticket and exit when the fee is paid. Instead, we had the honor system. The honor system worked like this: one asshole (me), running the entire lot from a shack two football fields up a hill from the entrances and exits. Our honor system was not a system at all. It was an opportunity for anyone who wanted to try to avoid paying to do just that. In the parking lot, the customer pulls into the lot, parks, gets out of their vehicle, walks up to me in the shack, pays their fee, and heads back to their vehicle to put the ticket I gave them on their dashboard. This system opened up the floodgates for people, especially those 150 yards away from the shack, to park and run off to their destination without paying. My job was to process payments for every person who parked, while keeping an eye on the parking lot to ensure nobody ran off without paying the five dollars. I challenge you to try to keep track of who has paid, as fifty cars are pulling in at the same time.

I had an excellent, state of the art, technique to prevent people from running off -- a scream out the window of "EXCUUUUUUUUUUSE ME! YOU HAVE TO PAAAAAAAY TO PARK HEEEEEEERE!" Some people would just look at me, defiant, and continue to run off, while others would yell "WHAAAAAAT?!" So, then I was engaged in a conversation from 150-200 yards away. It was delightful. It was like Prince Spaghetti day every day,

"ANTHONYYYYYYYY!" For you younger folks, check out the Prince Spaghetti commercial on YouTube and you'll get it! These "runners" would bolt out of their car doors, like when the starting gate opens at the Kentucky Derby. Before I could even yell, they were across the street and out of sight. Others ran crossing routes down the street, across bus stops, and through other parking lots to avoid being seen. Routes so good that, if I drew them up and presented them to any NFL team, I probably would have been offered a job as the offensive coordinator. Some other people, who chose not to run, were quite creative, parking and then crawling between cars to try to avoid being seen and paying that hefty five-dollar parking fee. The struggle each and every day to capture all the revenue took its toll on me.

I really believe that the parking lot was the only manned parking lot in the history of parking lots that had no enforcement of payment. The enforcement consisted of screaming at violators from a shack window in an attempt to convince them to come up and pay. When that did not work, I placed a note on the windshield of the car, reminding them to pay when they returned. That is if I could figure out which car they exited. As you can imagine, this enforcement was not very effective. The owners of the parking lot were obsessed with revenue, yet had no policies in place to ensure everyone paid for the service. Their failure to beef up enforcement was in part because they did not want to make waves, as the owners are well known in town and did not want any bad press. But, in my opinion, their failure to implement any effective enforcement was also due to a lack of business acumen on their part.

The owners had a contract with a towing company who, when called, was supposed to arrive to tow cars that were illegally parked (e.g. had not paid or were left there overnight). The problem was, this towing company took hours to arrive and by then, the violator was usually done with their business and gone. So, in essence, the towing company was useless to me. I suggested many times that the owners look into a new towing company with a shorter response time. I was told "no" for about a year and a half. Then one day, some asshole parked without paying, left, and was blocking in five customers. When it took the towing company hours to respond, the owners actually agreed to look into a new towing company. One of the two owners was all set to sign the contract with the new towing company that would have greatly helped enforcement, but, at the last minute, her husband, the other owner, said they would not change companies because the current towing company did him a favor back in 1986. Yes, 1986. I shit you not. A company that was not living up to its contract could not be fired because it did the owner a favor somewhere around the time that baseball went through Bill Buckner's legs in the '86 World Series. That is what I was up against every single day. After the refusal to switch towing companies, I no longer yelled out windows, placed notes on cars or tried to enforce anything. I went right along with the honor system business model and simply took money from those who paid and turned a blind eye to those who did not. That strategy made my final few months there more tolerable.

Double Dipping

The parking lot has a "no in and out privileges" policy, which meant that once you drove out of the parking lot, your ticket was no longer valid. If you had to come back to the parking lot that day, you had to pay again. Most parking lots and decks operate this way, and it is effortless to enforce because once you pay the fee and the electronic arm goes up and lets you out, you are done. If you return, you know that the arm will not let you in without getting a new ticket that you will have to pay when you exit.

The parking lot where I worked did not have the technology of an electronic arm, and apparently without that visual cue, customers could not wrap their minds around the policy of "no in and out privileges." The customers felt that, because there was no physical barrier restricting their entry and exit, they should be able to come and go all day as they pleased. This was a bone of contention for just about everyone who parked in the parking lot. "No In & Out Privileges" was printed on each ticket, which of course, nobody ever read. So, after months of fighting with people about the policy, I begged the owners to have signs printed that I could post on the booth itself. They did, and it helped slightly, but at least a dozen people a day tried to come back into the parking lot using the ticket they used earlier that day. In a way, I felt bad for the customers because they had not planned on leaving and coming back. They got there in the morning, paid their five dollars, and then waited all morning in court for their case to be called, only to have the judge adjourn for lunch before their case was called. Now they had to come back in an hour and a half or so. Some customers understood and were willing to pay the five dollars again because they needed the break and wanted to go to lunch. Others screamed, yelled, cursed, and accused me of being a thief. Still others accused me of being in "cahoots" with the staff in the courts. In their minds, we had walkie talkies and I'd say to the court deputies, "Ok, break for lunch and make these fuckers come back and pay again, over," and they'd reply "roger that, break for lunch, over." Customers would plead their case to me trying to avoid having to pay again.

SIX FLAGS STUART: I have to leave and come back, do I have to pay again?

ME: Yes, sir, there are no in and out privileges. It is posted on your ticket and as you can see (pointing at all the signs on the booth) it is posted here at the window.

SIX FLAGS STUART: That is fucking ridiculous! I already paid! You people are double dipping thieves!

ME: I am sorry sir, I didn't write the policy, I am just the employee who enforces it.

SIX FLAGS STUART: Six Flags lets you come and go all day with the parking pass!

ME: I'm sorry sir, we aren't Six Flags, and you did not purchase a parking pass today, you paid a one-time fee.

SIX FLAGS STUART: Yeah, but Six Flags allows it, why don't you?

ME: I'll tell you what sir, when they put up a roller coaster on the town square, I'll let you go in and out on the same ticket.

SIX FLAGS STUART: Fuck you, you goddamn thief! I should call the Better Business Bureau!

ME: This is not up for debate. Have a great day sir.

39

At least Six Flags Stuart had a clue as to what "No In & Out Privileges" meant. One glorious morning I had this exchange with a young female customer:

PERPLEXED PATRICIA: *Staring at the "No In & Out Privileges" sign and almost crying.* OH SHIT! What am I gonna do now? OH NOOOOOOO!

ME: What's wrong?

PERPLEXED PATRICIA: I am screwed, that's what's wrong!

ME: Is there something I can help you with?

PERPLEXED PATRICIA: I forgot the court papers in the car, I need those papers!

ME: Are your keys locked in the car?

PERPLEXED PATRICIA: No, it says no in and out privileges on the sign, now I can't get my papers!

ME: Ma'am, no in and out privileges means you can't drive out of the lot and come back in using the same ticket

PERPLEXED PATRICIA: Are you sure? Are you sure it doesn't mean that I can't go in and out of my car? I need those papers! Am I going to get in trouble for going in and out of the car?

ME: Ma'am, I assure you that you can go to your car as many times as you like!

PERPLEXED PATRICIA: Thank God! You should really make that sign clearer and not scare the hell out of people!

ME: I'll be sure to make note of your suggestion.

This "no in and out" confusion and non-compliance went on all day, every day, for my entire tenure. There were, however, exceptions I made to this rule. I had regular customers, court employees, lawyers, and long term contractors working inside the court buildings who parked in the parking lot five days a week. Each regular customer was paying twenty-five dollars a week, over 100 dollars a month. So, if they needed to run out for something, or for lunch, I did not charge them when they came back to park again. It was a professional courtesy and a way to say thank you for their business. After all, they had other parking options in the immediate area, and I wanted to keep their business.

This was all fine and dandy until I took a day off and the co-owner, who was my backup (I use that term loosely), worked the day for me. She charged the regular customers a second time when they came back. Many of these regular customers were contractors who worked on a courthouse building renovation for eighteen months, parked at the parking lot every single day, even on weekends. These guys (they were all men) would need to run out for a can of paint, supplies, or to grab a bite for lunch, and the owner would hit them a second time for another five dollars. There also were court reporters, court administrators, and other court employees paying each morning who just wanted to go to lunch, and she'd hit them a second time for another five dollars. The owner was like Paulie from Goodfellas. She didn't want to hear anything, it was just "fuck you, pay me." Need to run out for paint? Fuck you pay me! Need to run out for supplies from the hardware store? Fuck you, pay me! You work in the courts and want to go to lunch? Fuck you, pay me! These regular customers would plead with her and tell her that I did not charge them a second time because they were there every day and she would respond "I'm not him, these are the rules." When I would come back after a rare day off or an even rarer sick day, I'd be bombarded by regular customers, angry that the owner had stuck it to them. I'd apologize and try to make light of her double dipping. I thought of the owner as the Leona Helmsley of parking. All that mattered to her was the money, she had no compassion for customers whatsoever. She saw customers in that parking lot as walking five dollar bills, not as human beings. Paulie would have been proud.

Next Stop, The Nut House

The shack I was confined to all day stood at the top of a hill. The parking lot was sloped and the building sat at the top of the highest point of the parking lot. This gave me a view of the entire parking lot, although there were plenty of blind spots. I also had a great view of the court buildings, and since the windows of the booth faced east, I would see the sun rise each morning. As part of my easterly view, just over the iron fence dividing the parking lot and the city's property, was a county bus stop. The bus stop had a park like feel, with a gazebo, park benches under the gazebo, lots of plants and shrubs, a few nice trees, a tall flagpole where Old Glory flew, and a dedicated monument of some sort. As the early morning darkness turned to daybreak each day, I would see the sun start to slowly rise, its rays projecting through the bus stop gazebo and the fabric of Old Glory. What a peaceful little place. With each passing moment, the peacefulness would fade, as cars started multiplying on the roads, people started pulling into the parking lot, and the county buses rolled up to the peaceful little bus stop park.

As soon as the bus doors opened, the world of peace and tranquility that I enjoyed for a while each morning would be gone in a flash. Most people who got off of the bus would go on their merry way to court, to work, or wherever they were headed that day. Some people, however, lingered at the bus stop for hours, sometimes for the entire day. Sound traveled so well from the bus stop that I could hear conversations taking place on the benches under the gazebo. Most of the conversations at the bus stop were not quiet and friendly ones. There were lots of arguments, yelling, fist fights, drinking, smoking, and a host of other activities going on down there. A lot of people who seemed mentally unstable hung out there all day and would just yell shit out loud, have arguments with themselves, punch themselves, or harass people walking by. I would watch and listen to the bus stop antics all day and think to myself that after another month or so at this job, I may be joining the fun down there. All day long I would see people running to the bus stop as a bus approached, yelling "stop the bus, stop the bus!" The bus drivers waited for nobody. If you weren't at the bus stop, ready to board, your ass got left behind. This infuriated so many people and made the already unstable even more unstable. Some people would scream obscenities, kick the trash cans, or throw bottles of water, juice or booze at the bus. It was really a sight to see.

One particular day, a lady in her early sixties wearing a yellow shirt, ran after the bus. She screamed the typical "Stooooop! Stoooooop!" while she was running from about fifty yards away. Of course the bus drove off without her. She let out a scream and yelled "the Lord is gonna strike your bus down with lightning!" She went on a five-minute rant about God, lightning, and how the bus would not be in operation after God struck it down.

She had missed the bus and apparently knew that the next bus was not scheduled to come for another twenty minutes. She headed away from the bus stop, toward the restaurant district of town to get a soda. Her throat must have needed some cool relief after that expletive laced rant. A few minutes later, I saw her, in her bright yellow shirt, heading back toward the bus stop, Diet Coke in hand, as the bus passed her and came to a stop. She was about twenty yards away from the bus and would have easily made it, except for my intervention. I yelled "lady in the yellow shirt, you dropped something!" She did not drop anything. I was just fucking with her. She had no idea where my voice came from, but she knew it was directed at her. She stopped dead in her tracks to look for what she dropped. As she's looking around on the ground, the bus drove away without her. She started her rant up all over again. "Motherfucker! Lightning is coming! You didn't wait!" Instead of just waiting there for the next bus, she walked off somewhere.

While she was gone, a panhandler came up to my booth from the bus stop and asked me for change. I told him "I don't have anything for you, but in a few minutes, a lady in a yellow shirt will be walking towards the bus stop. She probably has some change for you." He replied, "oh, thank you, thank you sir, I'll ask her." Right on schedule, the lady in yellow, who by now has already missed two buses, walked towards the bus stop with plenty of time to spare. When she was about thirty yards or so from the bus stop, with the bus now approaching, the panhandler stopped her for change. I watched her try to deke him like Wayne Gretzky would a rookie defender but he was determined to get a few spare coins. As she finally came to a full stop and dug in her purse for coins to give the panhandler for hire, the bus pulled away, without her, again. As that third bus pulled away, she threw her Diet Coke at the bus and yelled "FUUUUUCK IT, I'M WALKING!" The panhandler got his change, I got my laugh for the day, and she got her exercise. It was a win, win, win!

Beverly Hills Court

As you have probably already figured out, douchebaggery was rampant at the Parking Lot. A large percentage of the clientele did not graduate from charm school, finishing school or probably even high school for that matter. They were not the most polished people or those from high society. But regardless of their financial status, level of education or occupation, you might think that basic manners and courtesy would have been displayed, especially for those customers headed to court. They were already in some sort of legal jam. You would be wrong.

There were a few acts of douchebaggery that consistently rubbed me the wrong way. Smoking in my face and in spite of not one, not two, not three, not even four, but FIVE NO SMOKING signs topped the list. But, there's a whole chapter on that infraction, so we'll go to number two on the list of douchebaggerry and asshattery: idling in a vehicle within a few feet of my booth. After all, nothing says I'm ready to take on the day like an 8' x 8' shack full of exhaust, especially when that vehicle could park in 85 other spaces, nowhere near the booth and my lungs. The exhaust was considerably worse on a rainy or humid day -- when the air was thick and heavy, it would just linger.

One particular overcast, drizzly morning a giant pickup truck pulled into the lot. This truck, complete with the monster truck wheels, screamed "I have a small penis." There were only two other cars in a giant parking lot, but where did this douche nozzle decide to park? If you guessed a few feet from my booth, you win! With his truck idling, Runty Rod got out, came up to the booth and paid his five dollars parking fee. Then he climbed back into "Rodzilla" and just sat there. "Rodzilla" was my nickname for the motorized extension of his small rod. As a few minutes passed, more customers pulled into the parking lot and came up to pay. The cloud of truck emissions from Rodzilla was getting larger and thicker with each passing minute, so much so that some of the customers that came up to pay at the booth were coughing and complaining. The fumes were starting to get to me, so I figured I better go out there and say something.

ME: *Waving my hands and shouting over his loud engine to get him to roll down his window.* Excuse me sir!

RUNTY ROD: Yeah, what's up?

ME: Sir, can you please turn off your engine? The exhaust fumes are starting to overtake my work area and other customers have complained about the fumes.

RUNTY ROD: Is it a law that I can't idle? Is there a new law against idling?

ME: Sir, I'm really not sure about current idling laws, but I'm asking as a courtesy to me and to others, the emissions are really overtaking us.

RUNTY ROD: If it isn't a law, then just leave me alone, I paid my five dollars!

ME: Ok.... could you at least move away from the payment area so that we don't have to breathe the fumes in?

RUNTY ROD: *Rolling up his window as if to say, fuck off, conversation over.* No! Leave me alone!

I walked back to the booth, pissed off, and thinking of 101 ways to get even with this guy. I come from a long line of spiteful, vengeful Italians, including my Mom, otherwise known as "The

Master." I graduated from the School of Spite and Revenge with top honors many years ago and had only the best teachers.

As Runty Rod continued to sit there, idling away, I continued to help the other customers while thoughts of revenge danced in my head. Then, like a gift from the gods, "The Heat Is On" by Glenn Frey came on the SiriusXM 80s on 8 channel. That made me immediately think of the movie Beverly Hills Cop, which featured that song. There's a scene in Beverly Hills Cop where Eddie Murphy's character, Axel, stuffed a banana into the tailpipe of the police patrol car that was trying to tail him. The banana clogged up the exhaust system of the patrol car and caused the car to repeatedly stall, which enabled Axel to get away. Could this really work? This had to be a stunt that only works in the movies, right?

Once the morning rush was over, and Runty Rod had left Rodzilla, I started googling "banana in the tailpipe prank." Surely, someone out there had tried this. My research came up with mixed reviews on success, and shit, I didn't have a banana that day anyway. Of all days not to bring a banana! I started searching my booth for something else to ram into Runty Rod's tailpipe. As my eyes scanned the inside of the booth where I kept my supplies, they began to focus on the roll of aluminum foil, which I kept to use in my toaster oven. I had almost a full roll of foil. If I made a dense enough ball of foil and rammed it in the tailpipe with something, it just might work. I went outside to gauge the diameter of Runty Rod's tailpipe. I then went back inside the booth and made a thick, dense ball of foil that I estimated to be slightly bigger than Runty Rod's exhaust opening. Now, I thought, how do I do this without being seen?

I went outside with a broom in one hand and the big ball of aluminum foil in the other, trying to make it appear that I was heading outside to sweep up the parking lot. I got right next to Rodzilla, got down on one knee and placed the foil ball into the opening of the tailpipe. I could not push it in by hand because the ball was larger than the opening. So, I got down into a billiards stance, and just like Minnesota Fats, I cocked my cue stick (broom handle) back and forth a few times, ready for the shot of my life. I could have sworn I heard someone yell "get in the hole!" and "Baba-BOOOOEY!" off in the distance as I pushed that ball of aluminum all the way into Rodzilla's tailpipe. I had to be sure it was in deep enough, so I used every millimeter of broom handle, until I was holding it by the bristles. There, I figured that should teach that douche nozzle a lesson he won't soon forget. At least I hoped so!

Now the wait was on. Every few minutes I looked across the street to see if Runty Rod was coming back. Finally, around noon, I saw him crossing the street and heading back to Rodzilla. My first thought was to film the action, or perhaps lack thereof, but I had too many customers coming up to the window to film. So, I just watched. Runty Rod climbed into Rodzilla, put his seatbelt on, and turned the key. Rodzilla started up for a brief second or two and then stalled. He did not even get it into drive before it stalled. He tried it again. This time Rodzilla started up long enough for Runty Rod to get it into gear. He was backed in to a spot and was at the top of a hill, so he started to roll down the hill, probably thinking Rodzilla was in gear and running, but about halfway down the hill he realized it had stalled again. He placed Rodzilla in park, got out and popped the hood. He fiddled with all kinds of stuff under the hood, thinking he would jiggle something and fix the issue. He closed the hood and got back in

Rodzilla, turned the key, and this time Rodzilla started up for a few more seconds, then stalled once again. This, along with his questionable penis size, must have made Runty Rod angry because he tried once again to start his penile extension on wheels, this time by flooring the gas pedal. This caused Rodzilla to roar loudly and start, but not before shooting that tin foil ball out of the tail pipe faster than a Nolan Ryan fastball, narrowly missing two men walking by and then rolling away under some cars. The two pedestrians thought Runty Rod threw something at them and started yelling at him.

PEDESTRIAN: Hey man, what the fuck?! Why are you throwing shit?

RUNTY ROD: *Hanging out the driver's window, clueless that something just shot out of his precious Rodzilla.* What are you talking about? I didn't throw anything!

PEDESTRIAN: Fuck yeah you did, you threw a ball at us, almost hit us!

RUNTY ROD: I don't know what you're talking about, I'm leaving court, I don't have a ball!

PEDESTRIAN: *Walking towards Runty Rod.* You fucking asshole, get over here! I'll kick your redneck ass!

Now caught up in the action, and realizing that the heat was indeed on him, Runty Rod decided to make a break for it and gunned his engine, screeching out of sight as the two men discussed amongst themselves what just happened. Although it only caused Runty Rod a minor inconvenience and a small argument, I felt that I had gotten my revenge and, most of all, some much needed daytime entertainment.

Rodent Retribution

Over the course of my two years, two months and two days at the parking lot, many different people came to park there to go to court. People came to the court for a plethora of reasons. The most popular reasons people visited the friendly (or not so friendly) confines of the county courts were to pay or contest traffic violations, obtain or renew a concealed carry permit, to obtain a marriage license, report that they were the victim of identity theft, or go through the eviction process. I had a steady flow of both tenants and landlords reporting to court for eviction proceedings on a daily basis. Of course, I heard both sides of the landlord tenant saga, not that I ever even asked about their cases. Many customers felt the parking lot attendant was a good sounding board and a quality source for advice and sympathy. In the vast majority of these eviction cases, the landlords had to go through hell to evict a tenant who was many months behind on rent. In some cases, landlords even had to go through months of court proceedings to have squatters removed from their properties. This cost the landlords a lot of time and money. They missed work to be in court, could not collect rent from their properties, and, in many cases, had to repair damage to their properties caused by the shady tenants or squatters. Many of the landlords were exhausted, at the end of their ropes, and looking for a quicker way out than the court system could provide. In one particular eviction case, the parking lot attendant stepped in.

A middle aged couple came up to the payment window looking upset and stressed out.

ME: Good morning folks, how are you today?

LANDLORD LUKE: Could be better, we hate having to keep coming up here trying to evict a tenant.

ME: I'm so sorry, I hope things work out for you in there.

LANDLORD LAURA: Thank you, we do too. It's been months and we're still battling this. We can't take much more.

ME: I am so sorry you're going through a difficult time folks.

LANDLORD LUKE: If I told you what's going on, you wouldn't believe it!

ME: Try me, I have heard just about everything.

LANDLORD LUKE: Well, we own several properties and at one of them, someone posted a rental scam on Craigslist, advertising that the property was for rent. Although the scam didn't work, it let shady people know that the property was vacant, so a family just decided to somehow get in and start living there. It's been a couple of months. They changed the locks, we can't get in, and they have squatter's rights under the law and we have to go through legal channels to get them out. It has cost us rent, time off from work, and now it's going to cost us a bundle to go through the legal process!

LANDLORD LAURA: *Starting to cry.* This is a nightmare for us!

ME: Wow folks, I am so sorry.

LANDLORD LUKE: We appreciate you listening to us, we didn't mean to vent to you this morning.

ME: No worries, you folks seem like good people. You know what? I have an idea that can help you.

LANDLORD LUKE: Really? Do you know a good lawyer or someone who specializes in this sort of thing? Have you gone through this? We are open to any ideas.

ME: Well, I know plenty of lawyers, none that necessarily specialize in this sort of situation, and by law I personally cannot give out legal advice myself, but I can offer you a non-legal strategy that may work to get them out and have you take back your property.

LANDLORD LAURA: Really? We'd love to hear it!

I told Landlords Luke and Laura a story that took place at my residence in Long Beach, New York back in the summer of 2003. I had moved into a home I was renting in March 2002. It was a great house, just 3 blocks from the ocean. It was quiet and peaceful there for about a year until out of nowhere, in the summer of 2003, a construction crew showed up at the house next door and demolished the house to the ground. It sucked, but I thought to myself that under the city's laws, the crew could only work certain hours rebuilding the house and they probably would not be there working on weekends. Since I was at work all day, I would probably only have to hear them for an hour or two in the evening when I got home from work. I could deal with that.

My assumptions were completely off base. Although 7:30 am was the start time sanctioned by the city's law, trucks started rolling in at 6:00 am dropping off supplies, and crews followed suit and showed up before 7:00 turning on radios, hammering wood, jackhammering, etc. It became unbearable. Rather than start a confrontation, I called the city several times to report the noise that started well before the city's ordinance allowed. Whether they showed up to talk to the construction guys while I was at work, I'll never know, but the early noise did not stop. The house that they were rebuilding was no more than fifteen feet away from my bedroom window and this madness was getting worse by the day.

One morning, a Saturday morning nonetheless, my doorbell rang at 6:15 am. I staggered to my front door, still half asleep. I opened the door and standing there was one of the construction workers.

ME: Yeah, can I help you?

DEMOLITION DICK: Yeah, unless you want cement dumped on your cars, I suggest you move them out of your driveway so we can get in to pour cement.

ME: First of all, my car is in MY driveway. Second, if you need access to my driveway to get the truck in, all you have to do is politely ask. You don't have to come here with an attitude. Besides, I'm the one who should have the attitude since you guys are here more than ninety minutes early each day waking up the neighborhood, not to mention on weekends.

Demolition Dick walked away back to the house under construction. I went back inside to get my car keys so I could move my car into the street.

I moved the car and as I walked up the driveway to go back into my house I heard Demolition Dick mumble something to the other workers and they all started laughing. At that point, I snapped. I told them I was tired of their shit and that I would make life miserable for them.

DEMOLITION DICK: How are you going to make life miserable for us, we're the ones making all the noise with loud tools and machinery!

ME: Trust me, you'll see!

I went back inside seething and thinking of ways to make them miserable. I had to do something that was legal, something I couldn't get in too much trouble for or even arrested for. Then it hit me. I remembered a news story from when I was a teenager about the United States military using music torture day and night to get Panamanian dictator Manuel Noriega out of the embassy he was hiding out in after being indicted on drug trafficking charges. The U.S. military played loud, annoying music day and night until they smoked him out a day or two later. I certainly had the speakers to deliver more than enough sound to these guys just fifteen feet away. Now all I had to do was pick the music. Maybe Demolition Dick and his pals liked rap, or metal, or classic rock, so I could not go with any popular stuff. I finally settled on The Chipmunks Christmas song, you know the one about the hula hoop and them not being able to stand the wait until Christmas. Nothing is more annoying than that song, especially when it is ninety degrees outside. So, I moved my four powerful speakers into the bedroom windows facing the workers. I popped the Chipmunks CD into the CD player and set the CD player to repeat for that one, very annoying song. I turned the volume all the way up and let it play on repeat. I went about my business in the house, took a shower, had breakfast, watched the morning news, all while looking outside every so often to see how they were holding up out there. Initially it did not seem to bother the construction workers, they were actually laughing about it. But after a couple of hours, I could clearly see they were at their breaking points and they were no longer laughing. They tried turning up their little boom boxes, but those could not come close to drowning out Simon, Theodore and Alvin. By 1pm they angrily packed up and left. I wasn't sure if I smoked them out with six straight hours of the Hula Hoop song or if they had a short work day planned, so I figured I would wait until Monday to see what would happen. Monday came, and guess what, they didn't arrive until 8:00 am. I had the speakers set up and ready to go, just in case, but when I went out to my car to go to work, Demolition Dick, the guy who confronted me about moving my car on Saturday apologized about the early work hours and from that point on, the guys showed up at the appropriate time each day. The Chipmunks delivered justice and sent a message. Don't fuck with the munks!

Now, back to the parking lot. Landlord Luke and Laura stood there in amazement after hearing my chipmunk story. They still looked a bit unsure as to how my story would apply to their situation, so I had to spell it out for them.

ME: You do have outdoor electrical outlets at that property, right?

LANDLORD LUKE: Yes, by the front door and in the back of the house right off the patio.

ME: Do you have access to powerful DJ type speakers with a lot of bass?

LANDLORD LUKE: I don't think so, I mean we're older, we don't have that kind of equipment.

LANDLORD LAURA: Honey, Barbara's son does DJing, maybe we could talk to her.

LANDLORD LUKE: Oh yeah, didn't think of that!

ME: All you have to do is get on the property, preferably at night when these people want to sleep, and deprive them of sleep by blasting music until they cave in and leave. It may take a few nights, but I am sure it will work. I strongly suggest that Chipmunk Christmas Song. It is proven to work!

LANDLORD LAURA: What about the neighbors? They will call the police on us, won't they?

ME: Do you know the neighbors there? Can you talk to them before you do it?

LANDLORD LUKE: We know them all very well, we used to live at this particular property for 11 years before we moved and started renting it out. The neighbors are not happy that squatters are living there. We've explained the current situation over there to most of them.

ME: So, do you think they'd be on board with this?

LANDLORD LUKE: I think they would be if the result was good for everyone.

ME: Worth a try, right? Can't hurt!

LANDLORD LUKE: We really appreciate it; we are going to give it some thought. We don't want to ruffle any feathers in the neighborhood, but it is worth some consideration. Thanks so much.

ME: No problem, hope things work out either way.

As they walked away, I felt that although they found my story entertaining, there was no way this couple would have the balls to pull this Noriega chipmunk shit off. After all, it is not for everyone. It takes a vengeful, spiteful fucker like me to have the fortitude to pull off a Noriega stunt. But, a couple of weeks later, Landlord Luke of the landlord couple paid me a visit.

LANDLORD LUKE: Hey man, how are you?

ME: Great, but the bigger question is how are YOU?

LANDLORD LUKE: Great! We took your advice...

ME: NO WAY!

LANDLORD LUKE: *Laughing.* Yes! My wife's friend Barbara has a son that is a DJ, he brought all the equipment over and we set it up on the back patio one-night last week, around 10pm. Of course, we spoke with all the surrounding neighbors first and they were all ok with it.

ME: Oh my God, what happened? And, I have to know, did you guys use the Chipmunks song or something else?

LANDLORD LUKE: Yes! We used the chipmunks and he mixed in the Macarena! He even brought those flashing dance floor lights and pointed them at the windows!

ME: Barbara's son is a savage with those lights, he even took it up a notch! The Macarena would've gotten me out in five minutes! How long did it take to get them out?

LANDLORD LUKE: Well the squatters inside were yelling at us out the window for a while, but we could not hear what they were saying, because the music was so loud. We just yelled back at them and told them to call the police which we knew they wouldn't do, because they were there illegally. By 1:00 am they started filing out with trash bags full of their clothes, a microwave, and all kinds of stuff. The place was filled with garbage when they left, but at least we got control of the house back!

ME: They didn't have furniture? How many people were there?

LANDLORD LUKE: There were three adults and five children. They were sleeping in sleeping bags and living in shitty conditions, probably because it was free. I guess they figured they would be tossed out at some point and would lose their stuff. They probably didn't think they'd be leaving so suddenly though! I stayed at the property that night, didn't sleep, of course, and waited on the locksmith to come and change all the locks.

ME: I am so glad this ended well for you guys!

LANDLORD LUKE: *Reaching in his pocket for money*. I just wanted to thank you and let you know that it worked out. Let me buy you lunch.

ME: No sir, that is not necessary. Just knowing it worked out is rewarding enough!

LANDLORD LUKE: Seriously, I want to thank you, you won't let me buy you lunch?

ME: I appreciate the gesture, but, frankly, I don't get a lunch break and I brought snacks with me. But I really appreciate the thought.

LANDLORD LUKE: Your boss doesn't give you a lunch break?

ME: Nah, part of the job I suppose.

LANDLORD LUKE: *Laughing.* Do you want Barbara's son to go to your boss's house tonight?

ME: *Laughing.* No, I think Barbara's son did his job already!

LANDLORD LUKE: *Shaking my hand.* Really, thanks again!

ME: I'm so glad it worked out!

So as Landlord Luke drove away, I felt like I should leave the parking lot business and become a "fixer" of sorts -- open a small business where I would listen to people's problems and offer wacky, yet effective solutions. But deep down, I knew all the credit went to those silly Chipmunks. Because whether it's 2003, 2018, or perhaps sometime way off in the distant future, Simon, Theodore, and Alvin always come through, with or without help from The Macarena.

Repeat After Me

There was a very popular song in 1977 called "The Things We Do For Love" by a band named 10cc. The song is about the crazy things people do for love and the extreme measures they will take to prove their love. It was a top ten smash hit, in part, I think, because people could relate to the message of the song. The song was catchy and sort of romantic. In the not so loving confines of the parking lot, it is not what people will do for love, but rather what they will do to save five dollars and avoid the parking fee.

On a typical morning, the parking lot would be at full capacity by 9am. Most of the judges in the courts adjacent to the parking lot were all on the same schedule, which meant everyone would arrive at the same time for their scheduled court proceeding. This marvel of modern scheduling would have people fighting for parking spaces and panicking when the parking lot was full. Each morning, I did my best to process the customers in an expedient fashion so they could get inside on time. This was a challenge as droves of people arrived at the same time, and I had to process their payments and watch everyone that pulled into the parking lot to ensure they all paid their fee before they ran off to court. I also had to be sure each car was parked within the painted parking space lines and only taking up one space, because a car in multiple spots is a revenue loss and a bone of contention for someone late for court who cannot find a spot. Occasionally, I did not notice a car parked outside the lines because I was either too busy or because the multiple space violator was parked in a blind spot next to a very large vehicle. But, like clockwork, if a vehicle was in multiple spots and the parking lot was at full capacity, the frustrated customers who could not find a parking spot would scream at me and let me know all about the inconsiderate person who parked their vehicle in two spots. But, by that time, there was nothing I could do except leave a note, politely written or otherwise, on the windshield.

On one glorious morning, after being berated by a dozen frustrated customers regarding an inconsiderate parker, I went outside my little shack of horrors to investigate the egregious violation of parking lot policy. As I approached the 1990s Lincoln that was as long as a yacht, I immediately saw it was in two, almost three spots. I went back to the shack to look for something to write a note on. I had a flattened cardboard box from a case of credit card receipt tape that was about 12"x12" in size. I grabbed a black Sharpie and wrote: "ONE SPACE PER CUSTOMER FUCKO! YOU ARE AN INCONSIDERATE PRICK!"

I walked back out to the vintage 1990 double parked boat and placed the large cardboard sign on their windshield. I tucked it ever so slightly under their Desert Storm era dry rotted wiper blades to ensure a gust of wind would not blow away my eloquent message. A couple of hours later, a guy wearing vintage clothing approached the little shack of horrors with my oversized greeting card in hand.

FUCKO FLOYD: Excuse me, did you put this on my car?

ME: No sir, what does it say? Let me see....

FUCKO FLOYD: It says I am a fucko and that I am a prick!

ME: Oh, you must be the guy who parked in multiple spaces.

FUCKO FLOYD: What do you mean?

ME: The policy is one space per five dollars and you made dozens of people angry this morning when you parked in two spaces and they could not get a parking space. It must have been one of them who left the sign.

FUCKO FLOYD: *Starting to walk away.* Oh, I thought it was you.

ME: Sir, you owe five dollars for the additional space you occupied that I could not sell to someone else.

FUCKO FLOYD: That's crazy! You want an extra five dollars from me?

ME: No, I don't want an EXTRA five dollars from you, I want the five dollars for the EXTRA space you took up that I could not sell to someone else when we were full earlier.

FUCKO FLOYD: I was in a hurry, it wasn't on purpose! Can't you make an exception?

ME: I'll tell you what, if you repeat after me, I'll let it go.

FUCKO FLOYD: Ok, just repeat after you?

ME: Yes.

FUCKO FLOYD: Ok

ME: Ok, here goes, "I parked like a complete fucko, I'm ashamed, and I will never, ever do it again!"

FUCKO FLOYD: You want me to say that?

ME: Yes, if you don't want to pay the five dollars for the additional space you occupied, you'll have to learn your lesson somehow.

FUCKO FLOYD: Ok, what was it again?

ME: "I parked like a complete fucko, I'm ashamed, and I will never, ever do it again!"

FUCKO FLOYD: Ok, I parked like a fucker...

ME: *Interrupting.* No, it's FUCKO! And it's "complete fucko."

FUCKO FLOYD: Ok, I parked like a complete fucko, I am sorry and ashamed and I will not do it again, ever!

ME: Close enough.

FUCKO FLOYD: So, I'm good? I can go?

ME: Yes, sir, you can go now.

FUCKO FLOYD: *Holding up the cardboard Fucko sign.* Can you throw this sign away for me?

ME: I don't have a garbage pail in here, and it's best if you hold onto it as a reminder of what you did anyway.

Floyd left, sign in hand, not the least bit ashamed because he had saved five dollars by admitting he is a fucko.

The Florida Flyer

All too often, people parking at the parking lot felt compelled to try to drag me into some sort of controversial political conversations. I rarely took the bait, as I was pretty certain that I would disagree with most of them on most topics. Just an educated guess, I suppose. Most of the customers' t-shirts, bumper stickers, and hats made it clear where they stood on certain issues, and I wanted no part of discussing it with them, whether I agreed with them or not.

While I rarely got reeled into political, religious or controversial discussions, I did put my two cents in more than I should have when it came to issues of common sense. If I saw someone do something stupid, I just had to know their thought process and could not resist asking them "Why?" If someone came up to me with a clearly exaggerated, or even complete bullshit tale of sorts, I called them out on it. I just could not keep my mouth shut. Southerners, for the most part, really do not call people out on their bullshit. They may think you are completely full of shit, but they will rarely tell you that you are full of shit. They will smile and say something passive aggressive like "Well, bless your heart" or just talk about you once you are out of sight. People from New York, and from most of the Northeast, will let you know you are full of shit, an asshole, or whatever else is on their mind. When I left the North and relocated down South, it was difficult to find that social filter when you are conditioned to have no filter. I do try to have a filter when dealing with friends, coworkers, and people I meet casually. But when it came to people who rubbed me the wrong way at the parking lot, I had no filter whatsoever, and I had no boss or supervisor sitting there regulating what I said. It was no holds barred each and every day.

On a rainy spring morning around 7:30 am, a middle-aged woman pulled into the parking lot and parked. She was one of the first cars in that day. I noticed she had Florida plates. That is something I noticed all day working in the parking lot, license plates from everywhere. She came up to the booth to pay and the following conversation took place:

ME: Good morning ma'am, how are you today?

AMELIA ASSHAT: I'm ok, a little tired. I had a long drive from Florida this morning to be here.

ME: Oh wow, glad you made it safely here in this rain. What part of Florida did you come from?

AMELIA ASSHAT: Thanks, I drove from Tallahassee.

ME: Oh wow, that's a hike. That's about 300 miles from here, right?

AMELIA ASSHAT: Yeah, I think GPS said 288 or close to it.

ME: You must've been on the road at like 3:00 am, you probably need coffee, there's a deli right around the corner.

AMELIA ASSHAT: No, I left at 5:30 am.

ME: Huh? 5:30? Oh, you must be from Tallahassee but started your trip from someplace closer today, right?

AMELIA ASSHAT: No, I left from Tallahassee at 5:30 am.

ME: Isn't Tallahassee like four or four and a half hours away?

AMELIA ASSHAT: I made it in two hours.

ME: *Knowing that I should just let it go, but....* Unless you were in a plane, you couldn't travel almost 300 miles in two hours, you'd have to average close to 150 miles per hour the whole way.

AMELIA ASSHAT: I made it in two hours. I was in the car, were you?

ME: I don't think I'd want to be in a car going 150 miles per hour for two hours, that's some Back to the Future stuff right there!

AMELIA ASSHAT: I didn't go 150 miles per hour, I went about 70!

ME: Ok.... so 70 miles per hour times four hours is 280 miles, you said GPS said it was 288, so it is about four hours travel time.

AMELIA ASSHAT: Why is this concerning you?

ME: I am not really concerned; I just was having a conversation with you until you brought something up that wasn't mathematically possible.

AMELIA ASSHAT: It is possible, I am here and I left at 5:30 am, end of story!

NEXT IN LINE LEO: *Chiming in.* Who drove 150 miles per hour?

AMELIA ASSHAT: NOBODY!

ME: This lady is claiming she drove 288 miles in two hours which would be an average of almost 150 miles per hour!

NEXT IN LINE LEO: Where did she come from?

AMELIA ASSHAT: I came from Tallahassee, Florida and I made it here in two hours.

NEXT IN LINE LEO: *Laughing.* Ma'am I think you're mistaken, there's no way you can get here from there in two hours!

All five people waiting on line then joined the discussion, agreeing that there was no way to drive from Tallahassee, Florida, to the parking lot we were standing in, in two hours.

Amelia Asshat stormed off, knowing deep down that she was completely full of shit, while the rest of us continued on with the conversation about her absurd claim.

NEXT IN LINE LEO: Why would she even say that? Was it going to impress you?

ME: People are full of shit all day up here.

NEXT IN LINE LEO: I would have just let it go and laughed about it later on.

ME: I wish I could sir, I wish I could.

Amelia Asshat came out of court a few hours later, at 1:20 pm, and as she passed by my booth on the way to her car I yelled "Safe travels, if you hurry, you'll make it home by 3:00 pm!" She said nothing, but gave me a one fingered farewell as she pulled away into the afternoon mist.

In Other Words....

We all have a song or two that we've sung over the years, only to find out that the lyrics we were singing were not the actual lyrics to the song. It happens, because some lyrics are difficult to hear clearly with the music playing, some lyrics simply sound like other words, some lyricists sing too quickly, and sometimes we just flat out get it wrong.

At the parking lot, the lack of English language comprehension went far beyond misheard song lyrics. It was an everyday occurrence to hear mispronounced words, made up words, and poorly substituted words. These are some of my favorites:

GARY GAZOO: Yo, where is the closest bus stop? I gotta catch a bus to Atlanta.

ME: Sir, the bus stop is right at the gazebo on the other side of that iron fence where the American flag is flying.

GARY GAZOO: What da' fuck is a gazoo?

ME: No sir, the GA-ZEE-BOW, that round structure where the American flag is.

GARY GAZOO: I ain't never heard of no gazoo!

ME: No sir, it is not a gazoo, it's a gazebo. Gazebos are in parks; some people have them in their yards. It is an open structure with a roof on it just like the one across the way. That's where the bus stop is.

GARY GAZOO: Why did you have to bring up gazoo? You couldn't just say over there? Ain't nobody know what a gazoo is!

ME: Sir, where are you getting gazoo from? He was a character on the Flintstones. You are heading to the gazebo.

GARY GAZOO: What's this about Flintstones?

ME: The Great Gazoo was a character on the Flintstones, he was a little green Martian that visited Fred and Barney, and....

GARY GAZOO: *Loudly interrupting.* Oh yeah, I remember Goonies! He was funny! Man, you bringin' back them memories with all this Goonies shit! I'mma head over to the bus now, you know when the bus comes up at the gazoo?

ME: No sir, I don't have a bus schedule, but hopefully you won't be waiting too long.

GARY GAZOO: Thanks man! Now I gotta Google or YouTube them Goonies when I get home, I remember how funny Goonie was!

ME: Ok sir, have a great day!

This discussion had just gone from 18th century pavilions, to cartoon Martians, and ended with a 1985 box office hit. The Great Gazoo always greeted Fred and Barney with "Hello, Dum Dum." In this case it was "So long, Dum Dum!"

While we are talking about outer space, the solar eclipse was a big deal around the country in August 2017. Here in the metro Atlanta area, we were gearing up for 97 percent coverage of the sun that August afternoon. Excitement was in the air, even at the parking lot.

ME: Good Morning sir, how are you?

ELLIPTICAL ERIC: Great! Hey, you gots any of dem' elliptical glasses for sale?

ME: What are you looking for sir?

ELLIPTICAL ERIC: Dem' elliptical glasses.

ME: *Knowing what he meant, but fucking with him.* Oh, they make glasses to go on elliptical machines now?

ELLIPTICAL ERIC: Huh? Machine? You gotta see the elliptical through a machine? I thought you just put dem' glasses on?

ME: Well, we only sell parking here, not any glasses, elliptical or otherwise.

ELLIPTICAL ERIC: Maybe you don't know what I mean. I wanna watch dat sun thing later, they say to get a pair of dem' elliptical glasses to see it.

ME: OH, the eclipse? You want eclipse glasses?

ELLIPTICAL ERIC: Yeah! Elliptical glasses! You selling those?

ME: No sir, we don't sell eclipse glasses, we are just a parking lot.

ELLIPTICAL ERIC: Where can I get dem' elliptical glasses at?

ME: The eclipse is today, so I am not sure at this point.

ELLIPTICAL ERIC: *Turning around and asking random people.* Do you know where I can get dem' elliptical glasses?

At least he wasn't my problem anymore. And, by the way, the 'elliptical' was majestic later that afternoon. Speaking of majestic, the people who misread court names were so much fun!

ME: Good Morning Sir, how are you?

HIS MAJESTY: Where's the courthouse at?

ME: Which court are you heading to today so I can point you in the right direction?

HIS MAJESTY: There are different courts?

ME: Yes, sir, there are several different courts and several different buildings.

HIS MAJESTY: Ummmmm…. I think it's majestic court!

ME: *Knowing he meant magistrate court, but why not fuck with him too?* You sure it is majestic court, sir?

HIS MAJESTY: 100% sure! I'm going to majestic court. I got accused of writing bad checks, so I gotta appear in majestic court.

ME: You sure it is not magistrate court, sir?

HIS MAJESTY: Nah, majestic!

ME: It is definitely magistrate court, sir. That's across the street on the corner.

HIS MAJESTY: Ok, but where would majestic court be?

ME: See that beautiful castle off in the distance, on top of the hill?

HIS MAJESTY: No, where's it at?

ME: I am kidding sir, there is no majestic court, it is magistrate court.

HIS MAJESTY: I think you're wrong. Hold on, hold on…I'm calling my wife!

HIS MAJESTY: *Talking on the phone.* Honey, what court am I going to today?

HER MAJESTY: Majestic court.

HIS MAJESTY: That's what I thought, the guy here's telling me there's no majestic court!

HER MAJESTY: Whaaaaaaat? It's majestic court baby, trust me!

HIS MAJESTY: That's what I thought, see you later!

HIS MAJESTY: *Turning back to me.* You heard that, right? It IS majestic court!

ME: You are both mispronouncing it sir, it is magistrate court. It is across the street.

HIS MAJESTY: I don't think you're right, but I will go where you tell me.

ME: Ok, good luck in there.

His Majesty exits magistrate court two hours later.

HIS MAJESTY: You were right!

ME: About?

HIS MAJESTY: There is no Majestic court!

ME: *Sarcastically.* Really?

HIS MAJESTY: Yeah, them security guys laughed at me when I asked for majestic court!

ME: I figured you meant magistrate court.

HIS MAJESTY: You was right! I shoulda' listened to you!

ME: Well now you know for next time.

His majesty rode off into the sunshine in his lavish 2003 Toyota Camry. I'm certain he felt relief as he looked into his rear view mirror and saw majestic court getting further and further out of sight. His day in that most palatial of courts was behind him. As for his bad check writing days, well, that remains to be seen.

The Irish Bobcat

My regular customers at the parking lot were really great people. I got the opportunity to get to know many of them on a first name basis and we always had some good conversations. We would talk about family, our jobs, the weather, sports, music and a host of other topics that were not too deep or personal. There were, however, a few customers that offered TMI, as the younger crowd calls it. Unsolicited, very personal information shared at a shack window in a parking lot can be a tad awkward.

A gentleman named Ron parked at the parking lot every Friday morning for the entire two plus years I worked in the parking lot. Ron was probably in his late 50s, perhaps early 60s. I'm pretty certain he was in some kind of weekly program offered by the courts, but I never got too personal by asking him the reason for his weekly visits. He was always pleasant to me and we would talk about work, the creepy guy that ran the parking lot across the street and a bunch of other casual topics. One particular Friday, which also happened to be St. Patrick's Day, Ron pulled in at his usual time and proceeded up to the booth.

ME: Hey Ron! Happy St. Patrick's Day!

RON: Oh yeah, it is St. Patrick's Day, isn't it?

ME: Sure is, but I thought you knew that since you're wearing green today.

RON: Nah, just a coincidence.

ME: Not a big St. Patrick's Day fan?

RON: Not so much anymore, but I had some wild St. Patrick's Days back in the day!

ME: *Laughing.* Oh really?

RON: Oh yeah! Every time St. Patrick's Day comes around I think of 1979.

ME: Good year for you?

RON: I don't know about the whole year, but St. Patrick's Day 1979 was great!

ME: *Wondering, should I even ask? Oh what the hell, the cat is almost out of the bag anyway!* What was so great about St. Patrick's Day, 1979 Ron? Fun times?

RON: Well, I was at a bar here in town and I was dancing on the dance floor. You remember that song "I Will Survive" by that black woman, don't remember who sang it...

ME: Gloria Gaynor.

RON: Huh?

ME: Gloria Gaynor sang that song.

RON: Oh yeah, Gloria Gaynor! Anyway, I am on the dance floor and I see this beautiful woman really cutting up the dance floor! Sexiest woman I ever saw! So I finally had the courage to go up to her and start dancing.

ME: Were you a good dancer Ron?

RON: Not really, but I had a few in me! I got her off the dance floor after "I Will Survive" and bought her a drink. I started telling her about myself and vice versa.

ME: Getting pretty interesting here Ron....

RON: Oh yeah! She asked what I did for a living, where I lived, and all that. I told her I lived with Jessie.

ME: Uh oh, was Jessie your girlfriend?

RON: NO! Jessie was my bobcat.

74

ME: Wait a second, back up Ron...you lived with a bobcat?

RON: Oh yeah, Jessie was great! So when I told this girl about Jessie, she didn't believe me. She wanted to go home with me to see Jessie, my bobcat.

ME: It's a shame I am married Ron, because that would be my new pickup line if I were single. "Hey, wanna come back to my place and see my bobcat?"

RON: *Laughing.* That's a good one!

ME: *Not really wanting to know.* So I take it the story doesn't end there, does it Ron?

RON: Oh nooooo! I took her back to my place and she saw Jessie. She really liked Jessie! She petted her and really took a liking to her! We had some more drinks and things started getting frisky!

ME: That's great Ron!

RON: As I was trying to get her bra off, she asked me why I named the bobcat Jessie and not whiskers or something that relates to a feline.

ME: And why did you name her Jessie?

RON: Well, it was really Jessica, but Jessie for short. I named her after Jessica Lange the actress. Had a big crush on her in the 70s.

ME: Ummmmmm....ok.

RON: Yeah, so she was amazing.... God she was beautiful, what curves! I still think about her!

ME: Who......Jessie?

RON: No, the girl I brought home! We had sex all night!

ME: *Cringing.* Oh, that's great Ron!

RON: I'll never forget her!

ME: Did you date her after that unforgettable St. Patrick's night?

RON: No, when I woke up in the morning she was gone! It was back to just me and Jessie. I never saw the girl again.

ME: That's sad Ron.

RON: No, not at all. What a wild night! We did things that most farm animals don't ever get to do! She liked to....

ME: Ok Ron, I got it....

RON: All night long! All night! That's what St. Patrick's Day reminds me of!

ME: Can I ask one question about that night?

RON: Sure! Ask anything you want! But I'll tell you right up front, she was about 5'5, what a rack! An ass you could bounce quarters off of....

ME: *Wondering why anyone would bounce quarters off someone's ass.* No Ron, I was just curious, was Jessie in the room during this all night romp?

RON: You know, I don't remember. But Jessie had free run of the house so who knows.

ME: How long did you have Jessie?

RON: A few more years, then she got too big. I gave her to a sanctuary.

ME: What a shame, you lost your wingman, I mean wingcat.

RON: The ladies loved Jessie! Well, I better get inside. Now I am in the St. Patrick's Day mood!

As Ron walked away, the lyrics from that Gloria Gaynor song entered my head, and how fitting they were in that moment. "Go on, now go, walk out the door, just turn around now, 'cause you're not welcome anymore." I never looked at Ron the same way again.

Dude, Where's My Brother's Car?

If you survived Y2K on New Year's Eve 1999 and safely made it into the year 2000, you probably remember a movie called "Dude, Where's My Car?" It was a mild box office success starring Ashton Kutcher. After enjoying a bit of fanfare at the box office, the film achieved cult-like status because it aired so frequently on cable television. The phrase "Dude, Where's My Car?" also became a pretty commonly used pop culture expression back in the early 2000s.

Fast forward 18 years, and the general premise of the movie -- a couple of guys hungover with no recollection of the previous night and the whereabouts of their car -- held true at the courthouse parking lot. A middle aged woman, obviously high on something, approached the payment booth one breezy spring morning.

ME: Good morning ma'am, how are you today?

TOOTHLESS TAMMY: *Tightly clenching two e-cigarette devices.* Why the fuck won't they let me in the court with these?

ME: I believe it is because there have been incidents of battery explosions with those devices in recent months. The courts recently started prohibiting them.

TOOTHLESS TAMMY: How the fuck was I supposed to know that? We come all the way from Macon! I don't know rules up in these parts!

ME: It'll be ok, just place them in your car and re-enter the courthouse.

TOOTHLESS TAMMY: Easy for you to say! My brother drove me here, he's inside the court. His case is being heard, I don't have his keys!

ME: Sorry about that ma'am, not sure what to tell you.

TOOTHLESS TAMMY: Can you hold them for me inside there?

ME: No ma'am, for starters we cannot hold personal property, and based on the fact that they explode, I don't think an 8' x 8' wood shack would be a great place to store them. Today's not the day I want to be incinerated.

TOOTHLESS TAMMY: Oh for Christ's sake, do you believe everything the media tells you? They don't explode! Fake News! Faaaaaaake Fuuuuucking News!

ME: Ma'am I've actually seen video footage of them exploding, but that's beside the point, we do not hold personal property in here.

TOOTHLESS TAMMY: *Now in full scream mode.* WHAT THE FUUUUUCK AM I GONNA DOOOOOOOO?! I GOTTA GET BACK INSIIIIIIIIIIIIIIDE!

ME: I am so sorry ma'am, perhaps you can hide them in the bushes and go inside and get the car keys from your brother and then put them in the car.

TOOTHLESS TAMMY: No, I can't be running all over the fucking place! I'm just going to put them UNDER my brother's car!

ME: *Wanting to rid myself of this nut job.* Ok ma'am, do whatever works best for you.

Toothless Tammy wandered off into the parking lot to place the explosive devices underneath her brother's car, which was also her ride home. Thinking I was rid of her, I carried on with my morning. All was quiet for a few minutes until Toothless Tammy suddenly appeared at the window once again.

TOOTHLESS TAMMY: What kind of car does he drive?

ME: What kind of car does who drive?

TOOTHLESS TAMMY: My brother Buck!

ME: Ma'am, how would I know what kind of car your brother Buck drives, I don't know your brother.

TOOTHLESS TAMMY: Well he paid you the goddamn five dollars this morning didn't he?

ME: If he's parked here, yes he paid, but I don't log in customer's names, car models, and information like that. I just give the customer a receipt to place on the vehicle dashboard.

TOOTHLESS TAMMY: Could be a green Toyota! Did a green Toyota pull in here today?

ME: Ma'am, didn't you ride here with him today?

TOOTHLESS TAMMY: Of course I did! That's a dumb question! Where's Buck's car?

ME: Then how do you not know what kind of vehicle you rode in this morning to get here? You came from Macon and were in the car for over 100 miles!

TOOTHLESS TAMMY: *Mumbling to herself and rocking back and forth.* Black Honda Civic, green Toyota, I'm so confused. Fuck fuck fuck.

TOOTHLESS TAMMY: *Now screaming.* WHERE'S MY BROTHER'S CAR?! WHERE'S MY BROTHER'S CAAAAAAAAAAAAR?! IT'S GOTTA BE FUCKING HEEEEEEERE!

ME: *Realizing this woman needed 24/7 supervision.* I suggest you ditch those e-cigarettes in a bush and go find your brother and stay with him until it's time to leave.

Toothless Tammy then started asking anyone who passed by "What kind of car does my brother drive?" and "Where's my brother's car?" hoping someone would just so happen to know Buck, and what vehicle he drove to court in that day. She also asked random strangers to place her e-cigarettes inside their cars until she was finished with court. Surprisingly, nobody took her up on that most normal and well thought out request. Toothless Tammy's investigation into the whereabouts of her brother's vehicle went on for another fifteen minutes or so. Finally, she decided to scamper off to court. I wasn't sure where she placed those e-cigarettes so that she could gain entry into the courthouse. And at that point, I really didn't care. I figured all was well with her gone, unless, of course, I heard an explosion under some random, poor bastard's car.

Toothless Tammy and Buck walked out of court a few hours later. They proceeded to get into Buck's white Ford Escape SUV, parked across the street in another parking lot. Dude, she found her brother's car! The end, right? Of course not! Buck and Toothless Tammy drove over to my parking lot and pulled up to the booth.

BUCK: *Yelling out the driver's side window.* You got my sister's e-cigarettes?

ME: No sir, I told her I couldn't hold personal items for her.

BUCK: Then where are they?

ME: You'll have to ask her sir. She didn't know what kind of car you drove, didn't know where you parked and I suggested that she place them in the bushes so she could get back into the courts. She also mentioned that she was going to place them under a car somewhere.

TOOTHLESS TAMMY: *Screaming from the passenger side window of that white Ford, having a complete meltdown.* Those are goddamn expensive! Where are my fucking e-cigarettes!? Ask him Buck, ask him! Where are they Buck, where are they?!

BUCK: Where should we look?

ME: I guess under cars and in bushes.

Out of nowhere came a woman pushing two small children in a double stroller.

STROLLING SARAH, *holding Toothless Tammy's e-cigarettes wrapped in a tissue, as not to directly touch those vile devices*: Do you know who these belong to?

ME: Where did you find those?

STROLLING SARAH: Tucked under my windshield wiper blades.

Toothless Tammy somehow managed to see the e-cigarettes through the potpourri of bird shit, dirt, and pollen on the windshield of the white Ford and ran toward Strolling Sarah, yelling "Thank you, thank you! I've been looking all over for these! I lost them this morning!"

Buck and Toothless Tammy drove away, puffing heavily on their newly discovered e-cigarettes as I explained the entire saga to the hero of the day, Sarah, who was shocked. I had to know one thing, the curiosity was killing me, so I asked the stroller pushing hero:

ME: What kind of car do you drive?

STROLLING SARAH: It's parked right over there, that red Volkswagen Beetle, why do you ask?

ME: *Shaking my head.* Well, she thought her brother parked here in a black Honda Civic or a green Toyota Camry, when in fact he parked across the street in a white Ford SUV, but then she put her e-cigarettes under the wipers of your red Volkswagen Beetle.

STROLLING SARAH: *Laughing.* Makes sense.

ME: Parking Lot logic, ma'am, parking lot logic. Thanks so much for your help!

There has been talk of a sequel to "Dude, Where's My Car" for quite a few years now. Supposedly, the existing script for that sequel is titled "*Seriously* Dude, Where's My Car?" I think "Dude, Where's My Brother's Car" or "Where the Fuck Are My E-Cigarettes, Buck?" would be much better options. If you're reading this Ashton, get in touch!

Turtle Troubles

I've watched more episodes of Judge Judy than I'd like to admit. Although she can be obnoxious at times, I've always enjoyed her approach and how she gets right to the point. She utilizes common sense and calls people out on their bullshit. Judge Judy, born in Brooklyn, New York, brings a New York, no nonsense attitude to her courtroom. One of my favorite Judge Judy catch phrases is "Where did you think you were coming today?" She uses that line often, usually to those dressed inappropriately for court or to those that are totally unprepared to present their case. I cannot tell you how many times that phrase ran through my head while working at the parking lot. I saw so many people arrive there on their way to court in pajamas, beachwear, and bedroom slippers, like it was the norm. I also saw people arrive to court with no plan for the animals in their vehicles or in some cases, for their own children's care while they were in court. It's almost as if the court dates that they'd known about for weeks, and in some cases months, just came upon them by surprise.

One late summer morning, people starting exiting the courts around 11:45 am. This was pretty typical as judges and court staff break for lunch and court is recessed until 1:00 pm or so. As people started getting into their vehicles and driving away, I heard a scream coming from one of the parking spaces occupied by an old, beat up pickup truck approximately thirty feet from my booth. "Where is he!" screamed a young man in his 20's accompanied by two similarly aged males. "Oh my GOD, I don't know! Holy shit, he's gone!" shrieked one of his companions. All three, visibly upset millennials, quickly approached my booth and stood at the payment window.

DONATELLO: Ok, where is he?

ME: Where is who?

DONATELLO: Our turtle!

ME: *Laughing*. Ok, funny...now seriously what's up?

RAPHAEL: Our turtle is gone! Do you have him in there?

ME: I don't even know what you are talking about. What turtle?

DONATELLO: You, or someone, stole our turtle! He's worth a lot of money!

ME: Excuse me sir, I have no fucking idea what you are talking about. This seems like some dumb joke.

MICHAELANGELO: It's no joke, we had a huge turtle named Cecil in the back of our pickup truck and now he's gone! He's over a foot in diameter and weighs about fifty pounds!

Donatello moved to the side of my booth and peered through the large glass door looking for their hard shelled friend inside my booth.

DONATELLO: I don't think he's inside that booth, I would have seen him.

ME: Why would I have your fifty-pound turtle in my tiny workspace?

RAPHAEL: He didn't mean you took it, maybe someone turned him in to you.

ME: Again, you truly have me at a loss. Why would you leave a turtle in the back of a pickup truck?

DONATELLO: He's our pet!

ME: Yeah, you've kind of made that point, but why wouldn't you leave him home rather than bringing him to a parking lot on a hot summer day?

DONATELLO: They are used to heat. Don't you know anything about turtles?

ME: I must've been out sick the day they held a training class for the parking lot attendants about turtles and their care.

RAPHAEL: Can you call the police to report the theft of our turtle?

ME: It's up to you to call the police if you feel something was stolen from your vehicle. It says right on your parking stub that we are not responsible for damage to, or theft of or from, your vehicle while in the parking lot.

DONATELLO: This is bullshit! No place is safe anymore! Not even the parking lot across from the courthouse! Cecil is gone!

ME: Maybe he wasn't stolen, maybe he got out of the bed of the truck.

DONATELLO: No way man, no way! How is a fifty-pound turtle going to climb out of a truck bed? No way possible!

ME: *Sarcastically.* I forgot, you're the turtle experts. On any account, I feel really bad for the turtle. He shouldn't have been in that truck to begin with. I hope you find him.

RAPHAEL: Thanks, we are going to call the police now.

The three angry and upset turtle lovers walked back to their pickup truck where they huddled and planned their next course of action. Donatello dialed the police while Raphael and Michelangelo stood in the back of the pickup bed, looking under tarps and various other items that were piled in there. As I watched them all come to terms with the fact that they'd never see Cecil again, something cast a strange shadow under a car about fifteen spaces down the hill from where they were parked.

The shadow was round in shape and moving ever so slowly underneath a Toyota Rav4.

ME: *Yelling out the booth window.* I think I see your turtle! He's under a car down the hill!

RAPHAEL: What?!

ME: I think your turtle is under a car, down at the bottom of the hill!

Now, everyone in the parking lot who was unfamiliar with the turtle turmoil was staring at me in bewilderment.

DONATELLO: Where do you see him?!

ME: Under that red Toyota Rav4 SUV at the bottom of the hill!

All three took off running down the hill towards the Toyota. As they approached the vehicle I heard a loud cheer coming from that general direction. They had recovered Cecil! The three young men started jumping up and down in a semi-circle, similar to a family that had just won the bonus round on Family Feud. Donatello struggled, but managed to hoist 50 pound Cecil in the air triumphantly as they all screamed "Wooooohooooo!" They slowly paraded Cecil up the hill, still cheering and screaming, and placed Cecil back in his redneck habitat. Donatello, now out of breath, ran back up to my booth:

DONATELLO, *breathing like he just carried a fifty-pound turtle up a hill*: Thank you man!

ME: Glad it had a happy ending.

DONATELLO: I guess he was able to get out of the truck after all! I never would have thought! Thank God he has a protective shell!

ME: *Sarcastically.* Yes, I thank God each day for shells.

Donatello started walking away just as a police car pulled up to the booth. Apparently the joy of recovering Cecil made them forget to cancel their report of a stolen and missing fifty-pound turtle.

DONATELLO: Are you here for the turtle?

OFFICER YERTLE: What turtle?

DONATELLO: The stolen turtle?

OFFICER YERTLE: I'm here because of a reported theft.

DONATELLO: Oh, we called but the turtle wasn't stolen, he was walking down the hill.

OFFICER YERTLE: I have no idea what you're talking about, but are you saying you placed the call and no longer need us?

DONATELLO: Yes, Cecil was found under a car.

OFFICER YERTLE: *Looking perplexed.* Ummmmm...ok then.

Officer Yertle stepped on the gas pedal with purpose, screeching his tires a bit as if to say "I want no part of this clusterfuck." Donatello, Raphael, Michelangelo, and Cecil drove away jubilant as I looked at the clock and thought to myself "Still 3.5 hours left of this bullshit today." Time sure does move like a fifty pound turtle when you're not having any fun.

The Intercepted Interview

There are lots (pun intended) of life rules out there that many people follow, such as: Be comfortable in your own skin; Drop the resentment within; Appreciate what you have and don't compare yourself to others. But much bigger than a life rule is The Golden Rule, "Do unto others as you would have them do unto you." Treat people the way you would like to be treated. Pretty simple, right?

At the parking lot, I always treated everyone with respect and offered a nice greeting and a willingness to help -- no matter how stupid the question or the person. I went above and beyond my job description on a daily basis to ensure that the parking lot was a welcoming place for everyone. After all, many arrived there headed to court and already stressed out about what they may face when they walked through those courthouse doors. I kept that in mind and went out of my way to be polite and even lent an ear when they wanted to vent about their situation. Many of my repeat customers commented on my demeanor and willingness to help. I was a good actor. I was almost always in a bad mood because of the working conditions, lack of help, lack of owner involvement, and the twenty percent or so of the customers who were just flat out rude and confrontational. That's where I drew the line. I took no shit from anyone and gave it back just as hard, if not harder, than they gave it to me. After all, I answered to nobody. The owners were not involved, and frankly, not interested in all the confrontations that took place daily. The pile of cash at the end of each day was their only concern. So, I ran things my way.

On a very busy and rainy Tuesday morning around 10:05 am, a woman pulled into the lot while chatting it up on her cell phone. She proceeded to run over the cones I placed in the parking spot next to my booth. She honked her horn in one long, steady, and obnoxious honk while waving her credit card out the driver's side window. I ignored her. This is not how the system worked. There was no drive-thru service at the lot. It was up to the customer to find an available (not coned off) parking space and then come up to the payment booth, where I was stationed, to pay. The incessant honking went on for several more minutes until she realized it was getting her nowhere. She then decided to come up to the booth while still deep in conversation with someone on her cell phone.

INTOLERABLE INTERVIEWEE: Didn't you hear me honking?

ME: Yes, ma'am, but we don't process payments at vehicles, oh and you ran over two traffic cones as well.

INTOLERABLE INTERVIEWEE: What cones?

ME: The ones wedged under your car.

INTOLERABLE INTERVIEWEE: *Talking into her phone.* Hold on.

INTOLERABLE INTERVIEWEE: *Now talking to me.* It's fucking raining, I have an interview, you could have come out to help me! What the fuck do they pay you for?

ME: Ma'am that's not how it works, I cannot leave my post. There is money in here and I don't have a portable credit card machine to process your payment at the car.

INTOLERABLE INTERVIEWEE: Just take the card and do your job then! Can't believe exceptions aren't made in the motherfuckin' rain! Now I'm going to be wet for my interview!

ME: Ever hear of an umbrella ma'am?

INTOLERABLE INTERVIEWEE: I have an umbrella in the car!

ME: Lot of good it's doing you.

INTOLERABLE INTERVIEWEE: You are fucking rude! Just run the card!

ME: I'm only rude to people who show no respect and think they're entitled.

Intolerable Interviewee resumed her phone conversation as I was processing her payment. She ranted about me, asking her cell phone buddy "Can you believe this asshole here? Did you hear that shit? What kind of service is this?" She went on to tell the person on the phone that she had a job interview at the probate court at 10:30 am. She also mentioned who she would be interviewing with.

ME: *Sarcastically.* Thank you ma'am, good luck on your interview! Don't forget your umbrella!

INTOLERABLE INTERVIEWEE: I should have you fired for making me come out in the fuckin' rain!

I ignored the now very wet, Intolerable Interviewee and watched as she sloshed back to her vehicle. She sat in her car for a few more minutes and continued to chat it up on the phone very loudly, still ranting about the service she felt she was entitled to. Then it hit me. I had her name from the credit card slip, I knew where she was interviewing, and who she was interviewing with. I could not let this information go to waste! I pulled up the court directory on my laptop, and bingo! I found the interviewer's name. I picked up the outdated, landline phone, dialed *67 to block the number from being seen on caller I.D., and dialed the number.

INTERVIEWER: Mrs. Mary Jones speaking, how can I help you?

ME: Ummmm yes, Mrs. Jones, do you have a Lisa Smith coming in at 10:30 am for an interview today?

INTERVIEWER: I really can't give out any type of information like that, may I ask who you are?

ME: A concerned citizen.

INTERVIEWER: Can I ask what you need or what this is in reference to?

ME: Yes, it is in reference to Lisa Smith who is coming in to interview with you in a few minutes. I would think twice about hiring her.

INTERVIEWER: I can't confirm that I have an interview with a Lisa Smith, but if I did, can I ask why I should not hire her?

ME: Of course. Lisa has a very difficult time exercising common courtesy. She has an entitled mentality, thinks she's better than other people, talks down to people, shows little respect, and is not fit to deal with the public. And what a filthy mouth Lisa has too! I just want to save you the time and trouble Mrs. Jones.

INTERVIEWER: Can I ask how long you've known her?

ME: Long enough Mrs. Jones, long enough. Take my word for it. Lisa Smith is more drama than an episode of Real Housewives! Spare yourself.

INTERVIEWER: *Laughing*. Ok, well thank you for the heads up, I'll keep this in mind.

ME: Just looking out for you and the court system, you don't need her ass parked (hint hint) in your office each day, you'll go insane!

INTERVIEWER: Ok, well, have a great day! Thanks for the information.

ME: You as well Mrs. Jones!

It was approaching 10:20 am and the Intolerable Interviewee, umbrella now in hand, jumped puddles over to the courthouse for her now tainted interview. I felt I did my part; the rest was up to Mrs. Jones inside the courthouse.

A few short minutes later, at 10:28 am, I saw the Intolerable Interviewee headed back towards her vehicle. I thought to myself, how could an interview be finished two minutes before it was scheduled to start? Did she forget something? Of course, the Intolerable Interviewee was back on her phone, spilling the beans about what just happened inside. "Why the fuck did they make me come all the way here if the position was filled? Waste of my fucking day! Yeah, yeah, they said they forgot to call and cancel! Unfuckingbelieveable!" The Intolerable Interviewee, still ranting on her cell phone, backed out over the traffic cones and headed out of sight. For that one rainy morning, me and Mrs. Jones, we had a thing going on, and that was to teach the Intolerable Interviewee the Golden Rule.

Corporate Complaints

As with any business, the parking lot was not exempt from people wanting to lodge complaints to a higher, corporate level authority when they felt the rules there did not apply to them or that my enforcement of those rules was not legitimate. Little did they know that no such higher authority existed at the parking lot. Sure, I did not own the business, but the owners wanted no part of handling complaints or dealing with unruly people, so I had to get creative and deal with them myself. In an irate, complaint fueled person's eyes, I was just a mere, uneducated, minimum wage earning parking attendant. How could I possibly give them the answers they wanted, the remedies they needed or the parking justice they sought? Some of those pillars of society wanted, and in many cases demanded, the phone number to the corporate office. Was this suddenly Bloomingdale's? What corporate office? For almost a year, I tried to explain to the foul mouthed, red faced, temper tantrum throwing demographic of the parking business, that no such office existed and that I had the final say. Surely, there HAD TO BE someone higher up the parking corporate ladder than me they insisted! Unfortunately, there wasn't. I insulated the owners from all the bullshit and stood on the front lines each day handling the complaints, and there were many!

A year into the job, the owners decided that they were going to install Wi-Fi inside the booth. This was a welcome addition, as I enjoyed streaming music and now it would not be eating up my monthly cellular data. The day after the Wi-Fi was installed, the owners informed me that they not only got Wi-Fi, but they got the package which included internet (Wi-Fi), phone, and cable television, because it was a cheaper deal than just internet alone. I initially thought it was a waste, because I knew for certain that I could not (or would not) sit and watch TV with all the crap that transpired each day in that parking lot. I had to be on alert the entire time I was on duty. I also thought that a landline phone was a waste, I mean who still used a landline? But then it occurred to me that the landline could be the answer to my prayers when it came to irate customers that demanded they have a corporate office number to call! They now had someone else to speak to, or so they thought!

First things first, I knew that the owners were not going to provide me with an actual landline phone because they barely provided anything. Most of the supplies to run the business came out of my pocket. I headed over to Wal-Mart and purchased a fifteen-dollar cordless phone. I brought it into work the next day and set it up. I got the landline phone number from the paperwork the installer had left and dialed it from my cell phone. Sure enough, it rang! The corporate office was just about open for business! I then called the bank that processed the credit card transactions and asked them to program the credit card machine so that the new phone number would appear on all receipts. Within minutes, we went from no corporate office, to a fully staffed executive suite just waiting for the first complaint to be lodged. It didn't take long.

A couple of days later, a loud mouthed cell phone conversationalist came up to the payment window right in the thick of the morning rush. I was trying desperately to communicate with her and get her, and those waiting behind her, on their way. She gave me the "wait a minute, don't interrupt me" finger as the line behind her continued to grow and she continued this all important speaker phone conversation about her upcoming court case.

ME: I'm sorry ma'am but we have to keep the line moving, will you be paying by cash or card?

BELLIGERENT BERTHA: I thought I told you to wait a motherfuckin' minute!

ME: Ma'am, if you're not ready to pay and want to continue your phone conversation, please be polite and step aside so that the others can be taken care of and can get on their way.

BELLIGERENT BERTHA: Who da fuck are you, tellin' me what to do?

ME: I'm in charge here and those are the rules, if you don't like them, you can leave and park someplace else.

BELLIGERENT BERTHA: *To her phone companion.* I'mma have to call you back.

BELLIGERENT BERTHA: *Now to me.* Who da' fuck do you think you are talkin' to me like that?

ME: Ma'am, it is rude to be on the phone yapping away while a line of people are waiting!

BELLIGERENT BERTHA: Fuck all y'all! You don't pay my motherfuckin' phone bill!

ME: It's not about who pays your phone bill ma'am, it is about common courtesy. If you can't be courteous, you need to leave.

BELLIGERENT BERTHA: Bitch, I ain't going nowhere! And I'm gonna call your corporate office! Gimme the motherfuckin' number! I'mma have your sorry ass fired!

ME: Gladly, ma'am.

BELLIGERENT BERTHA: Write down the owner's name and the phone number! What time do they open?

ME: Well, it's 8:45 am now, I believe they open at 10:00 am.

An hour and fifteen minutes allowed me enough time to get through the customers of the morning rush so I could field that maiden call from Belligerent Bertha to the corporate line and give it all the attention it deserved. So I wrote down the phone number that would call the shiny new Wal-Mart phone that was sitting inches away from me, as well as the name of my fake boss, Heywood Jablome (Hey-would Ja-blow-me), and handed it to Belligerent Bertha.

ME: Now will you be paying cash or card for your parking?

Belligerent Bertha tossed a five-dollar bill at me and stormed off, still angry that I asked her to show some common courtesy to other people. The next few people in line were appalled by Belligerent Bertha's behavior and expressed some mild sympathy for me. All in a day's work up here, I told them. The rest of the morning was not as eventful, that was until the corporate office phone rang at 11:08am. I thought to myself, let's have some fun with this!

ME: *In my best robotic voice.* Hello, you have reached the Parking Lot Corporate Office. Please say the name of the person you'd like to speak to.

BELLIGERENT BERTHA: Heywood Jablome.

ME: *In that same robotic voice.* I'm sorry, we didn't get that.

BELLIGERENT BERTHA: HEYWOOD JABLOME!

Now if Bertha was in public somewhere, the people around her were probably wondering why Bertha was asking someone to blow her.

ME: *Trying desperately not to laugh.* One moment please.

I let Bertha stew on hold for a minute, so I could compose myself after laughing.

ME: Hello, this is Heywood Jablome, how may I assist you?

BELLIGERENT BERTHA: Yeah, I am calling about your parking lot guy, the one by the courts.

ME: Oh, our courthouse parking lot downtown?

BELLIGERENT BERTHA: Yes, that one. The guy working there is so fuckin' rude! He told me to get off my cell phone and cussed me out this morning!

ME: I am so sorry to hear that ma'am; we have never had a complaint before.

Of course we hadn't, she was the first call to the splendid new corporate office!

BELLIGERENT BERTHA: Well, you GOTS one now!

ME: Ok ma'am, any idea what time were you there this morning?

BELLIGERENT BERTHA: What's that got to do with it?

ME: Well, I want to look into it for you.

BELLIGERENT BERTHA: Musta been about quarter to nine, somewhere around there.

ME: Can you hold for a minute?

BELLIGERENT BERTHA: I guess.

ME: Thanks, I'll be right back. (*Pressing mute and holding the phone in my hand for 30 seconds*).

ME: Hello, are you still there ma'am?

BELLIGERENT BERTHA: Yes, I'm here, I ain't got all day!

ME: Ma'am I just reviewed the tapes, are you wearing a white blouse, black pants, black shoes and carrying a beige purse?

BELLIGERENT BERTHA: UUUUUUUUUH......yeah, how'd ya know all of that?

ME: I just reviewed the security tapes and wanted to be sure I had the right person.

BELLIGERENT BERTHA: Yeah, that's me, now whatcha gonna do about your guy over there?

ME: Well according to the tape ma'am, you're the asshole, not him.

BELLIGERENT BERTHA: WHAT? What did you just call me?

ME: I said, you're the asshole, not him. You instigated the whole thing. You cursed at him, would not get off your phone and acted like a complete asshole. The tape does not lie, you should be ashamed of yourself!

BELLIGERENT BERTHA: Fuck you! I am never parking there again! What kinda shit is this?

ME: *Hanging up*. Good riddance ma'am.

Belligerent Bertha must have placed that call from somewhere near the parking lot, because she slowly walked past the booth about 10 minutes later while looking up at the security cameras I had mounted on top of the booth. They were three security cameras I had brought in a few months earlier from my garage that did not work, but I installed them on top of the booth as an asshole deterrent. Bertha did not utter a word to me, knowing her tale of bullshit had been debunked by Heywood Jablome at the non-existent corporate office, using the non-existent video tape from the non-functional security cameras. I could not wait for the next corporate complaint!

The next corporate complainer arrived early one afternoon, a week or so later.

IN & OUT IAN: *Flashing a previously purchased parking ticket.* I'm good, right?

ME: Hold up sir. Did you just arrive?

IN & OUT IAN: Well, yes and no. I was here this morning and I paid. I had to leave for a few hours and come back.

ME: I'm sorry sir, but once you leave the lot, your ticket is no longer valid. There are no in and out privileges. It is explained on your ticket and on the posted signs.

IN & OUT IAN: *Reading his ticket.* This is bullshit! You are going to take another five dollars from me?

ME: No sir, I am simply going to charge you for parking again.

IN & OUT IAN: I've never heard of this! This is robbery!

ME: Sir, if you parked in a parking deck and left, the electronic arm would not open and let you back in without paying again. Think of this the same way without the electronic arm.

IN & OUT IAN: What if I refuse to pay AGAIN?

ME: Then I will have no choice but to have your car towed.

IN & OUT IAN: You are a fucking thief! You're probably going to pocket the money!

ME: Sir, I don't make the rules, I'm just the poor slob who shows up for work every day and has to enforce them.

IN & OUT IAN: Well, I want the owner's name and phone number! I am beyond pissed off at you people!

ME: No problem, sir.

I wrote down the corporate number along with our infamous owner's name, Heywood Jablome, and handed it to him.

IN & OUT IAN: *Handing me his second payment*. I'm going to own this place when all is said and done!

ME: Ok sir, hope you have a good afternoon.

In & Out Ian's hands were shaking with anger as he walked away from the payment booth. He stopped in his tracks about 50 yards from the payment booth, pulled his phone from his pocket, and started dialing the number I had just given him. Afternoon court was about to resume and the lot was bustling with people heading back to court, but that did not stop In & Out Ian from seeking justice. The phone in my booth started to ring.

ME: Parking Corporate Office, how may I direct your call?

IN & OUT IAN: Yes, Heywood Jablome please.

ME: *Having fun with this*. I'm sorry sir, we must have a bad connection, can you speak up?

IN & OUT IAN: HEYWOOD JABLOME, PLEASE!

Now people walking by In & Out Ian are starting to stop and stare.

ME: One more time sir...what is it you need?

IN & OUT IAN: HEYWOOD JABLOME!

Now some people walked by In & Out Ian and laughed, while others had a very disturbed look on their faces.

ME: *Trying not to laugh.* That's disgusting sir!

IN & OUT IAN: Huh? Is he there?

ME: Is who here?

IN & OUT IAN: HEYWOOD JABLOME!

ME: I really don't care for your obscene request!

IN & OUT IAN: *Oblivious to the phonics of the name.* What request? I want to speak to the owner, Heywood Jablome!

ME: Oh! You want to speak to Mr. Jablome! Can you hold?

IN & OUT IAN: Hurry, I have to be in court!

ME: Heywood Jablome.

IN & OUT IAN: Who is this?

ME: *Turning the obscene request back on him.* Heywood Jablome, sir.

IN & OUT IAN: *Still not getting the Heywood Jablome pun.* Yeah, I got charged twice here at your lot!

ME: Did you leave the lot and re-enter?

IN & OUT IAN: Yes, but court was adjourned, it was not my fault!

ME: Sir, we have no control over court scheduling. We have a clearly posted "no in and out" policy.

IN & OUT IAN: So, you can't make an exception?

ME: No sir, I am sorry.

IN & OUT IAN: Fuck you thieves! I am calling the Better Business Bureau!

ME: Sir, if you are going to continue yelling obscenities I am going to hang up.

IN & OUT IAN: I'm just getting started!

ME: Ok, sir maybe there is something we can work out!

IN & OUT IAN: I demand a refund on both fees today for my troubles.

ME: I have something better in mind.

IN & OUT IAN: Great! What's that?

ME: Hey, would ya blow me?

I hung up the phone before I heard Ian's reply. While tears of laughter rolled down my face, the phone started ringing again. It was obviously In & Out Ian, who surely did not like my settlement offer. I yanked the phone plug out of the wall so it would stop ringing, at least on my end anyway. I needed a break from corporate calls and from my alter-ego Heywood Jablome. I left that day before In & Out Ian came back to his car. I never did hear from him again. But there were many more, not as comical, corporate complaint calls over my remaining time at the parking lot.

Roll Tide!

The Christmas season is my favorite time of the year. From the day after Thanksgiving, right up until Christmas day, there is a special kind of magic in the air. I really get into the holiday music, decorating, cooking, holiday movies and all that comes with that time of the year. I tried to bring that holiday spirit to the parking lot, hoping it would bring out the best in people, even if it was just for a month or so. I decorated the inside and outside of the booth, played holiday music, and put out a bowl of holiday candy for customers to enjoy. Just because it was a parking lot, it did not mean we could not have some spirit and joy there. I did not go "over the top" because I always kept in mind that some people that came to the parking lot for court appearances were going through a difficult time in the court system. But, I wanted everyone to feel welcome and to set a holiday vibe.

I immediately discovered that people, even during the holiday season, had to make an issue out of petty crap and rain a shit storm down on my holiday joy. After each transaction, I always thanked the customer and wished them a great day, no matter what time of year it was. During the holiday season, I would say happy holidays instead of have a great day, to keep it festive. I said happy holidays not as a slight to Christmas, but to cover all the holidays, including New Year's. Well, this was an issue for many. I was often accused of participating in a war on Christmas by saying happy holidays. A few days before Christmas, a pickup truck with Alabama tags pulled into the parking lot and parked at the top of the hill, just a few feet from my booth. An older couple got out of the truck and headed over towards me, with four teeth between the two of them.

BECKY SUE: Y'all opened up yet?

ME: Yes, we are open.

BECKY SUE: What time them courts open up?

ME: Eight o'clock.

BECKY SUE: Oh, we got 45 minutes! What are we gonna do for 45 minutes?

ME: There's a deli on the corner if you want to grab some coffee.

BECKY SUE: What's a daily? We ain't from 'round here.

ME: It's a deli, a small restaurant where they serve sandwiches and coffee and things like that.

BECKY SUE: *Talking to Billy Bob.* You wanna get coffee at that daily?

ME: It's deli ma'am, D-E-L-I.

BECKY SUE: Oh, I thought you said daily, you sound like that Tony Sopraner guy on the HBO.

BILLY BOB: We come all the way from Alabama, we ain't used to paying for parking!

BECKY SUE: We are here for fuckin' justice!

BILLY BOB: Becky Sue, he don't wanna hear you!

BECKY SUE: Piss off Billy Bob, don't tell me what to do!

BILLY BOB: How much we owe you?

ME: Five dollars, sir.

BILLY BOB: Here you go. Don't listen to her, she's crazy.

BECKY SUE: Fuck you Billy Bob, I ain't crazy!

ME: Ok, thank you folks! Hope you have a great holiday!

BECKY SUE: It's Merry Christmas now!

ME: Excuse me?

BECKY SUE: It's ok to say Merry Christmas now, that Muslim is out of office!

ME: It was always ok to say Merry Christmas, ma'am, I just say happy holidays or have a great holiday because people celebrate different things and it covers everything.

BECKY SUE: It's merry fucking Christmas where we are from!

BILLY BOB: Becky Sue, nobody wants to hear your nonsense, let's go to get the coffee.

Billy Bob and Becky Sue argued and fought the whole way to the daily, a.k.a. deli. A few minutes later I heard Becky Sue's voice coming from the corner as they were waiting to cross the street back to their truck. Of course, they had to stop for another chat with me.

BECKY SUE: That deli guy said happy holidays too, what's wrong with you people here in Georgia? It's Merry Christmas! Trump is here to save Christmas!

ME: Ok ma'am, Merry Christmas.

BECKY SUE: We are here for justice! *Looking up at the sky.* Lord, rain that justice down! Rain your justice! Let the holy water rain on down!

ME: I hope everything works out for you today.

BECKY SUE: We are fighting for our rights! Fighting for our rights, just like Trump is fighting for Christmas!

ME: Best of luck.

BECKY SUE: You don't need luck with the Lord on your side!

BILLY BOB: Becky Sue, he don't wanna hear this, let's go to the truck.

BECKY SUE: We have to tell our story. Let justice reign down, oh Lord!

BILLY BOB: Becky Sue, keep our business private!

BECKY SUE: Them drugs weren't my son's! Those cops planted them. Crooked cops here in Georgia, planted drugs on my son!

ME: I am sorry to hear that ma'am.

The parking lot started to fill up, but Becky Sue was going nowhere. She wanted to be sure everyone knew about her son, about the alleged crooked cops in Georgia, and about the war on Christmas. She yelled out "WE ARE HERE FOR JUSTICE! LORD RAIN DOWN JUSTICE!" at anyone who passed by. She stopped random people and told them all about her son's case, as Billy Bob pleaded with her to stop and go inside. Finally, Billy Bob got through to her and they left the parking lot and proceeded inside. I turned my holiday music on to try to rid the area of the negative energy Becky Sue had spread. An hour or so later, like a poltergeist, Becky Sue was baaaaaaack!

BECKY SUE: Nothing resolved, we gotta come back in February!

ME: Well, take care of yourself and Happ..., Merry Christmas!

Billy Bob climbed into the driver's seat of the truck and started it up, but Becky Sue wasn't ready to go yet. She stood on the passenger's side of the truck and hollered at anyone who would listen to her. She wanted the entire State of Georgia to know her son had been wronged. Billy Bob was screaming at her to get in the truck. Finally, after 20 minutes of ranting, Becky Sue opened the passenger door and started to climb into the truck with her now, completely aggravated husband. As "Sleigh Ride" from The Ronettes played loudly on my radio, Billy Bob prematurely and impatiently put the truck into gear and gunned the engine while half of Becky Sue's body was still outside of the truck, sending Becky Sue rolling end over end, fifty yards or so down the hill while screaming and calling Billy Bob every expletive under the sun. Billy Bob drove down the hill to recover Becky Sue. Billy Bob was rattled and ran over to aid Becky Sue, who was shaken up. He helped her up off the ground as Becky Sue punched him repeatedly in the face. Just like Becky Sue, Billy Bob's truck now started to roll down the hill. He forgot to put it in gear when he hopped out to help his beloved wife. Billy Bob ran after his rolling redneck ride and managed to bring it to a stop just before taking out a city lamp post. People from all corners of the lot descended upon Becky Sue and Billy Bob to ensure they were ok. No sooner did Becky Sue get her wits about her, then she started telling her new found audience all about her son's court case and about the injustice he faced while dusting the dirt and grime from her tattered clothing. When Becky Sue finally had her fill of holiday storytelling, she climbed into the truck, completely this time, and she and Billy Bob took that road before them, and maybe sang a chorus or two. After all it was lovely weather for a sleigh ride together with Sue. Merry fucking Christmas indeed Becky Sue, merry fucking Christmas!

Your One Stop Shop

"One stop shop" was coined at an auto repair store sometime in the late 1920s as a new and unique marketing strategy. Almost one hundred years ago, auto parts, auto repairs, and auto sales were all new and separate businesses. That is until the business model of the one stop shop came into play. As of the late 1920s, customers could now go to one place, instead of three, to satisfy all of their automotive needs. Even way back then, when cars were still a novelty, few wanted to drive all over town for related goods and services at multiple locations. Since that catchy phrase went into play, many other businesses in other industries have adopted the same phrase. It has been used so often that "one stop shop" became a cliché of sorts. Fast forward almost one hundred years to the age of Amazon.com where someone can not only find any item they need or desire, but can buy it without leaving their home or office. For those who choose to leave the home or office, big box retailers such as Target and Wal-Mart are "one stop shop" meccas where one can buy anything from batteries to underwear, and then get tonight's dinner.

I've parked in thousands of parking lots during my life at baseball games, concerts, train stations, and hundreds of other venues. It never occurred to me to ask the parking attendant to sell me anything other than a parking space. But apparently, people have gotten so used to the ease and convenience of the "one stop shop," both online and at brick and mortar locations, that many assume every business is now a "one stop shop" even a parking lot. On almost a daily basis I was peppered with strange purchase requests.

One hot summer afternoon an older gentleman pulled into the parking lot. He parked in the parking space directly in front of my booth. He exited his minivan, and opened the back hatch. He pressed a button inside his vehicle and an electric ramp lowered a mobility scooter onto the pavement of the parking lot. He raised the ramp and locked his vehicle. He then attempted to drive over to me on his electric scooter to pay for his parking. For some reason, his scooter was not starting up. He fiddled with it for about ten or fifteen minutes before finally giving up and pushing his scooter over to me at the payment window.

ME: Hi sir, good afternoon! How are you today?

FREDDY FUSE: *Pointing at his scooter.* I want to pay for that parking space and I'll take a scooter fuse for this here model.

ME: I'm sorry sir, what is it that you need?

FREDDY FUSE: I need to pay for my parking and I need a fuse for my Pride Victory 9 scooter.

ME: I am sorry sir, we don't sell scooter fuses.

FREDDY FUSE: Why the hell not?

ME: Ummmmm, because we are a parking lot.

FREDDY FUSE: But don't you have folks coming in on these here scooters? You should have the parts for them!

ME: Sir, we are not a store, we are a parking lot.

FREDDY FUSE: Then what do you have that damn 'house' that you are in for? Don't you sell stuff out of there?

ME: No sir, this is like an office, not a store.

FREDDY FUSE: For fuck's sake, now what am I gonna do?

ME: Where do you normally by your scooter fuses?

FREDDY FUSE: I think at an auto parts store. Is there one around here?

ME: Yes, sir, there is one just down the road, a couple of traffic lights up.

FREDDY FUSE: Ok, can you lift my scooter and put it in your house there? I need you to watch it while I am gone.

ME: I am sorry sir, but that won't fit in here and I cannot hold personal property.

FREDDY FUSE: *Using his favorite expression.* Oh for fuck's sake, now I gotta load it back in the car?

ME: How long are you going to be sir?

FREDDY FUSE: Probably just a few minutes.

ME: Why don't you just leave it on the side of my "house" here by the window and I'll keep an eye on it for you.

FREDDY FUSE: Ok, I'll be right back.

Freddy Fuse drove down the road for his scooter fuse and returned a few minutes later.

FREDDY FUSE: Ok, I am back.

ME: Did they have your fuse?

FREDDY FUSE: *Holding up a bag.* Yeah, I think this is it.

Freddy fumbled with the scooter fuse box on the side of my booth, just outside the window while grumbling his favorite "for fuck's sake" expression a few times as he was trying to replace the fuse. Suddenly, he was shouting.

FREDDY FUSE: YOU GOT A FUCKIN' RATCHET SET IN THERE?

ME: *Talking out the window.* No sir, I'm sorry.

FREDDY FUSE: You don't have anything in there do you? For fuck's sake, I need a ratchet set to get at the part!

ME: Do you have one in your car?

FREDDY FUSE: If I had one in the car, why the fuck would I be asking you?

ME: Ok sir, no need to get rude. It's not my fault you blew a fuse.

Freddy had blown more than one type of fuse today.

FREDDY FUSE: I'm not blaming you for the fuse blowing, I'm blaming you for not having what I need!

ME: *Sarcastically.* No problem sir, I'll be sure to take notes on everything that is requested and run it by management and perhaps they'll stock everything so everyone goes home happy.

FREDDY FUSE: *Missing my sarcasm.* Great idea! But it's not gonna help me now. I gotta get this scooter home and fix it in the garage, WHERE THERE ARE TOOLS!

ME: Ok sir, hope you get it fixed.

Freddy, now with a couple of fuses blown, pushed his impotent scooter back to his minivan and loaded it inside. Freddy feverishly drove out of the parking lot and headed home to his ratchet set. I sipped on my Vitamin Water and thought to myself "For fuck's sake, I need something stronger than Vitamin Water to get me through the rest of this day!" If only we sold booze.

Unfortunately, scooter fuses weren't the only items requested by parking customers.

ME: Hi sir, how are you today?

STATIONERY STEVE: Doing ok, thanks. I need to pay for my parking.

ME: Ok sir, are you paying by cash or card?

STATIONERY STEVE: Card, but I'm going to need a box of envelopes also.

ME: Envelopes?

STATIONERY STEVE: Yeah a box of 50 or 100, doesn't matter. Letter sized!

ME: *Rolling my eyes.* Ok, let me check the back.

STATIONERY STEVE: Ok.

I stood there staring at stationery Steve, in disbelief that he actually thought I sold envelopes in a parking lot, that I had various sized boxes for him to choose from, and that I had a "back" stockroom inside my 8'x 8' shack.

STATIONERY STEVE: Why are you still standing here, I thought you were going to check the back for the envelopes?

ME: What back?

STATIONERY STEVE: You said you would check the back for the envelopes!

ME: Sir, I was being sarcastic. Where is there a "back" to check inside this little room? We are a parking lot, why would we sell envelopes?

STATIONERY STEVE: As a convenience, I thought maybe you had a supply closet in there. You didn't have to be an asshole about it!

ME: You came to a parking lot, asked to buy office supplies from a parking attendant, and then believed there was an office supply stockroom in a tiny wooden shack, but I'm the asshole?

STATIONERY STEVE: Wow, you're fucking rude! Just let me pay for my parking!

ME: Not rude sir, just stunned.

Stationery Steve went on his way, without his coveted envelopes. He passed by about an hour later sipping on a soda from the deli around the corner. I couldn't help but wonder if Steve asked for a box of envelopes in lieu of fries with his sandwich combo. But who had time to wonder about Steve, I had to head to the back to take inventory of the office supplies.

It did not end with scooter fuses and envelopes. The most popular request was for auto parts, and I was even told by a gentleman that we should carry "a full arsenal" of auto parts for people who break down. I had to explain to him the business model and purpose of AAA. Some thought that because cars parked in our lot, we should provide parts so that those cars could be fixed, just in case they broke down.

One morning a man in a car pulled into the parking space right next to the booth. I was busy handling a line of customers, but once I got the line of customers processed and on their way, I looked over at that car and saw that nobody was inside. Great, I thought to myself, another person who ran off without paying that I'll have to deal with when he comes back. No sooner had I finished that pleasant thought, I noticed a man crawling on the ground, circling my booth. My initial thought was that this guy was looking for a way in to try and rob the place, so I was ready and on alert. After a minute or two passed, I decided to confront him through the window.

ME: Hey, sir! Can I ask what you're doing down on the ground out there?

AIR PUMP ASSHOLE: Just looking for the air pump.

ME: What?!

AIR PUMP ASSHOLE: Looking for the air pump, my tire light is on!

ME: Sir, why are you looking out there for an air pump?

AIR PUMP ASSHOLE: Oh, is it inside there with you? Hand me the hose through the window, I figured it had to be somewhere!

ME: Sir, this is a parking lot, not a service station. We do not have an air pump or compressor.

AIR PUMP ASSHOLE: Why the hell not?!

ME: I just explained that sir. We are a parking lot, not a service station!

AIR PUMP ASSHOLE: Yeah, but there are cars here, ain't there?

ME: Yes, sir, there are cars everywhere. People park at various places but air pumps are found at service stations, not in random parking lots.

AIR PUMP ASSHOLE: My tire is low! You don't have a bike pump in there?

ME: No sir, there are two gas stations down the street, less than a quarter mile from here. They'll have air pumps for you there.

AIR PUMP ASSHOLE: But it's gonna be flat by the time I get out of court!

ME: Then I suggest you drop the car off at the station so they can patch it while you're in court and then pick it up afterwards. It's walking distance.

AIR PUMP ASSHOLE: You can't patch it while I am inside?

ME: Again sir, I don't have pumps, patches, or anything that can fix your tire.

AIR PUMP ASSHOLE: Then what do you do here?

ME: I can tell you what I don't do, and that's fix cars or car tires.

AIR PUMP ASSHOLE: That's some real bullshit! If I owned this lot, I'd have people fixin' shit and helping people!

ME: I'll relay your visionary business idea to the owners next time I see them. Until then, the gas station is your only option.

Air Pump Asshole rolled away slowly on four bald tires, one of which was flat, in the direction of the service stations. Like Air Pump Asshole's tire, and because of all the bullshit that took place in that parking lot, I was utterly deflated. Unfortunately, there was no quick fix for me, not right at that moment anyway. My fix would come a few months later when I finally quit and got the hell out of there!

Sadly, it was not just products the customers felt we should carry. Many of these lunatics wanted specialty services, in addition to their parking spaces. One early morning, a woman took it to a whole new level.

RECYCLING RHONDA: How much for parking?

ME: It is five dollars, ma'am.

RECYCLING RHONDA: Does that cover me all day?

ME: Yes, ma'am, it is good all day, you just can't go in and out.

RECYCLING RHONDA: Oh, that's no problem, once I'm here I'm here. No plans on going anywhere.

ME: Ok great! Will you be paying by cash or card today?

RECYCLING RHONDA: I'll be right back!

ME: No problem.

I assumed Recycling Rhonda was going back to her vehicle to retrieve her cash or credit card, now that she knew the cost of parking. But, once again, this was the parking lot, and nothing was that cut and dry.

RECYCLING RHONDA: *Walking towards the payment window with a phone book sized stack of old magazines, newspapers, cardboard, etc., and placing it on the shelf outside my window.* I'll be right back with the cans and bottles!

ME: Huh? What is this? What cans and bottles?

RECYCLING RHONDA: My recycling, here is the paper, I'll go get the plastic and glass.

ME: Ma'am, you do realize where you are, right?

RECYCLING RHONDA: Yes! At the parking lot next to the courts!

ME: So, why would you think a parking lot across the street from a courthouse would want, or take, your recycling?

RECYCLING RHONDA: It's all the same, county owned stuff, no?

ME: Ma'am, first off, we are a privately owned parking business. We are not owned by the city or county. Secondly, even if we were, we would not take garbage here!

RECYCLING RHONDA: Why not?

ME: Because there are different county and city services offered at different locations. You wouldn't go to traffic court to adopt a dog from the county shelter, would you?

RECYCLING RHONDA: Apples and oranges!

ME: How is that apples and oranges? You coming here with your trash is just as ridiculous as trying to rescue a county shelter dog in traffic court!

RECYCLING RHONDA: Not even close! Ok, so what do I do with my recycling?

ME: You bring it home and put it out on the curb on recycling day!

RECYCLING RHONDA: When is that?

ME: Ma'am I don't know where you live so I suggest you call your township and inquire.

RECYCLING RHONDA: Can you give me the number?

ME: Try Google ma'am!

Recycling Rhonda stormed away, her pile of paper recyclables in hand. It was at that point that I realized I needed something stronger than coffee to get me through those mornings. While Recycling Rhonda Googled her local recycling schedule, I searched Amazon Prime for flasks.

The mother (pun intended) of all service requests came one summer afternoon.

ME: Good afternoon ma'am, how are you today?

MENTALLY MEAGER MOM: *Holding a baby.* You will be watching baby today?

ME: Excuse me?

MENTALLY MEAGER MOM: You will be watching baby?

ME: Ma'am, this is a parking lot.

MENTALLY MEAGER MOM: But I no bring baby into court, you watch?

ME: We do not offer childcare services at a parking lot, and you would just leave your baby with a stranger?

MENTALLY MEAGER MOM: You working here? You watch baby?

ME: Ma'am, perhaps there's a language barrier here or something but I do not watch children here.

MENTALLY MEAGER MOM: *Holding the baby up, as to hand him to me through the window.* I be one hour! How much?

ME: I don't think you understand, ma'am! Me no watch baby here!

MENTALLY MEAGER MOM: Oh, you no watch?

ME: No ma'am, me no watch.

MENTALLY MEAGER MOM: Who watch?

ME: *Pointing at Mentally Meager Mom.* YOU WATCH BABY!

MENTALLY MEAGER MOM: Oh, me no watch, me go to court!

ME: You can bring him in the courthouse, ma'am!

MENTALLY MEAGER MOM: You no watch one hour, maybe one half hour? I have diaper and juice in bag.

ME: NO! You bring him with you!

MENTALLY MEAGER MOM: *Pointing at baby.* He go in court?

ME: Yes, ma'am, he go in court!

MENTALLY MEAGER MOM: OOOOH! I thought no court for baby, you watch him. I bring him inside!

ME: Very good ma'am, you bring him inside.

The Mentally Meager Mom paid for her parking and carried her baby into court with her. I stood there stunned. I mean, I had been asked to watch dogs, ferrets, personal property, firearms, and a host of other things in the recent past, but now we had entered a whole new realm. I was hopeful that I had just been Punk'd and that the TV crew was going to hop out of the bushes laughing at me. The crew never came; it was all too real. Somebody was actually going to drop their baby off in a parking lot, with a complete stranger. Although this would be the most serious thing I'd been asked to do, the requests for add on goods and services continued on for the rest of my tenure at the lot.

For example, this is a list of other goods and services people requested, and assumed we provided, at the parking lot:

Goods: Scissors, tape, wrapping paper, tissues, aspirin, ibuprofen, candy, mints, gum, newspapers, magazines, bottled water, soda, coffee, hot chocolate, hot dogs, ice cream, sandwiches, umbrellas, jumper cables, tools, car batteries, socks, phone chargers, baby wipes, paper towels, ace bandages, air fresheners, slim jims, cigarettes, chewing tobacco, and my all-time favorite, A MAP OF ATTRACTIONS so they could see all that the city had to offer on one convenient, easy to read brochure.

Services: A baby changing station, copying and collating, faxing, restrooms, an ATM, phones, Wi-Fi, computer access kiosk, check cashing, car washing, oil changes, legal advice, pet sitting, and, as you just read, child care.

Donuts and Karma

During my two plus years at the lot, I had the innate ability to determine whether it was going to be an average day of assclownery or a full blown day of douchebaggery, within the first few minutes of arriving at work. There was just a feel in the air, I really cannot explain it. I knew what was coming, but all I could do was hold on and pray for mercy. My only morning solace was my visit to Dunkin' Donuts on my way into work each morning. I got to know the crew there well through my conversations with them each day. We'd joke about dealing with the public; we felt each other's pain. I was at Dunkin' Donuts so early each day, they'd see me pull in and they'd start making my large iced coffee. They had nicknames for me like boss and chief. Going to Dunkin' each morning took my mind off what was waiting for me twenty minutes or so down the road. So, if the assclownery started at Dunkin', twenty minutes away from the lot, you knew it was going to be one long and fucked up day.

For some reason, Fridays were very busy at Dunkin', even at 5:45 am. At 5:45 am Monday through Thursday, I was the only guy in the place. But on Fridays, office workers stopped by to load up on dozens of donuts for their places of business. Perhaps it was a TGIF ritual at these offices to get everyone loaded up on sugar and ready for the weekend. On one rainy Friday, I pulled into an almost full Dunkin' parking lot at 5:45 am. I thought, what the fuck are they giving away here today? I went inside and I was about the fifth person in line. The employees looked up at me and smiled and made a face as if to say "sorry for not having your coffee ready today!" I motioned back that it was no problem and waited my turn. It was a few seconds later that the first assclown of the day reared his ugly head.

DONUT DELIBERATOR DAVE: I'm going to need four dozen donuts, please.

EMPLOYEE: Sure, would you like me to mix them up or do you want to pick them?

DONUT DELIBERATOR DAVE: Oh! I'm definitely going to pick them all!

I was thinking to myself, ok he's going to pick a few kinds and take three or four of each. But as usual, my expectation of the general public let me down in a colossal way.

EMPLOYEE: Ok, go ahead.

DONUT DELIBERATOR DAVE: Ummmm...I'll have one cinnamon because that's for Janet in accounting, she hates chocolate. One glazed because Martha told me that the other donuts are too rich for her.

Now I am thinking, you have to be fucking kidding me! Is this fucko going to explain every fucking donut selection for four dozen donuts?

EMPLOYEE: Ok, what else?

DONUT DELIBERATOR DAVE: Ummmm...I'll have one of those green and red sprinkled donuts because it is festive for Christmas! Make it two of those! They're gonna love them! Oh, and you have red and green frosted too! Oh, so festive! I'll take two of those also!

Didn't this guy know that you could take a shit on a breakroom table at work and people would start asking for the crackers to spread it on? When food is free, people don't care or ask questions, and they certainly do not inquire about the donut selection thought process that took place earlier that morning. They grab armfuls of food and race back to their desks all while trying not to be seen or judged. Yet this madness at Dunkin' continued!

EMPLOYEE: Ok, what else?

DONUT DELIBERATOR DAVE: How many is that so far?

EMPLOYEE: That's only six donuts.

DONUT DELIBERATOR DAVE: Ok, I have a ways to go! I think Mark is a chocoholic! Can I have two double chocolates? Double the chocolate for Mark!

EMPLOYEE: Ok, what else?

A huge sigh of impatience was starting to be let out by the now seven people in line. People were huffing and puffing and looking at the time. I knew I'd have to step in soon.

DONUT DELIBERATOR DAVE: *Pointing at the donuts with the huge "Boston Cream" sign over them.* Are those Boston Cream?

EMPLOYEE: Yes, sir.

DONUT DELIBERATOR DAVE: *Laughing.* I'll take one of those because Jim in receiving is from Boston, he'll get a kick out of it! He'll feel like he's back home!

ME: No he won't! Come on now!

Everyone on line and behind the counter looked over at me.

DONUT DELIBERATOR DAVE: Are you talking to me?

ME: Yes! Jim won't care about the Boston Cream donut just because he's from Boston!

DONUT DELIBERATOR DAVE: And why do you say that?

ME: Because it's a cliché and this is Dunkin' Donuts, you aren't at an authentic pastry shop in Boston! I'm from New York and if someone brought me a donut from Dunkin' just because it had a New York name attached to it, I'd laugh at them!

DONUT DELIBERATOR DAVE: You don't even know Jim or his sense of humor! Mind your own goddamn business!

ME: But I do know corny clichés when I hear them! Jim will smile when you tell him about the donut, and the link to Boston, and then he will call you an asshole behind your back to the other workers. Trust me! Spare yourself, and us! This is complete insanity!

Everyone on line and behind the counter laughed heartily, except of course, The Donut Deliberator.

DONUT DELIBERATOR DAVE: Just pick the rest! I don't want to be around rude people!

Donut Deliberator Dave grabbed his two bags containing two dozen donuts each and high tailed it out of the donut shop to the delight of the remaining patrons, but not before glaring at me on his way out. I gladly took one for the team so that we all could get on with the morning. After putting a stop to the donut deliberations, I came to terms with the fact that an even fresher hell was waiting for me just a few miles down the road.

The day that started with donut deliberations did not disappoint! When I arrived at the lot, the Wi-Fi service and the credit card machine were not working, there were beer cups all over the parking lot from the Thursday night hoopla at the bar around the corner, and a couple of cars that were illegally parked overnight. Once I got set up, got the fifty beer cups picked up and got

Comcast to fix my Wi-Fi, which also remedied the credit card machine, I settled in for a long day ahead.

A little while later, a silver BMW pulled into the now almost full lot. The driver backed his luxury vehicle into the spot furthest from the booth, down by the entrance, ever so carefully. I could not help but notice the pretentious, fake European license plate that was affixed to the front of the car. A few minutes, later a guy in his 30s wearing a grey suit and sunglasses (on a rainy day), got out of the European luxury car. He stood by it for a few minutes looking over his prized possession and buffing out the little dirt spots on it with a handkerchief while smoking a cigarette and talking on the phone. This slick continental dude then moseyed on up to the booth while still smoking and chatting on the phone. He started fumbling with the outdoor payment kiosk, ignoring the giant "PAY AT WINDOW" sign affixed to it.

ME: Sir, the sign says to pay at window, I can help you here.

KARMA COUNSELOR KENNY: Huh?

ME: The sign on that kiosk covering the screen says to pay at the window. And the five signs around me say no smoking, so please put out your cigarette.

KARMA COUNSELOR KENNY: Who the fuck are you to tell me what to do?

ME: I am in charge here, if you don't like the rules you can leave.

KARMA COUNSELOR KENNY: Fuck off, no asshole making minimum wage is going to tell me what to do or where to park!

ME: I'd rather be working here than coming to court.

KARMA COUNSELOR KENNY: I'm a lawyer asshole, I'll make more today than you make all year!

ME: I guess lawyers that can't read are in high demand these days.

KARMA COUNSELOR KENNY: I own a BMW, a 700,000-dollar house, 1000-dollar suits, what do you have?

ME: Class, something you have none of.

KARMA COUNSELOR KENNY: Just ring me up, you minimum wage making moron.

So this ambulance chasing asshole handed me his credit card, I processed his payment, and sent him on his way. The man on line behind him was shocked at how rude he was, almost apologizing to me for what the other guy had said. I told him it was no big deal and that I had a thick skin. While I had a lull in the action, I decided to Google the name of this so called lawyer that I had from his credit card slip. After a few minutes of googling, I pieced together that the name on the credit card was his father's, the named partner of the law firm, and that this guy was just some low level ambulance chasing douche nozzle working for Dad. I figured it was all over anyway, time to move on with the day. But, it is never over at the parking lot.

KARMA COUNSELOR KENNY: *Walking back to his car.* Hey asshole, what was I in there for, fifteen minutes max?

ME: And your point is?

KARMA COUNSELOR KENNY: I made 3500 dollars in fifteen minutes. How much did you make in the last fifteen minutes?

ME: 3500 dollars sounds about right for you.

KARMA COUNSELOR KENNY: Damn right it does!

ME: But, the bigger question is how many cocks did you have to suck in there for that 3500 dollars? What do you get per cock these days? Oh, and make sure you give your Daddy his credit card back when you return to the office!

Karma Counselor Kenny was completely stunned, humiliated and red faced as the people on line laughed at my one liners. He stormed back to his shiny BMW. As the light rain fell, Karma Counselor Kenny revved his engine and screeched out of the parking lot. As he got not more than one hundred yards or so down the street, he fishtailed on the wet pavement and crash his prized possession into a metal stanchion near the bus stop, rendering his fine piece of European craftsmanship undriveable. I laughed, and laughed, and laughed some more. I waved at him several times as he stood roadside on his cell phone while waiting for the tow truck to arrive, but, for some reason, I did not get a wave or greeting back. As his vehicle was lifted onto the flatbed wrecker, I realized that I witnessed something many of us never get to witness, which was karma. I know, we always say karma is going to get this one or that one, but how many times do we get to witness it mere minutes after someone had it coming to them? There was parking lot justice after all, and just like those red and green sprinkled donuts earlier that morning, it was just in time for the holidays!

Church Chicanery

I would be remiss to write a book about all the shenanigans that took place at the parking lot without talking about the church that was located right near my booth. It was a storefront church, not a traditional church like you picture in your mind when you hear the word church. If you were to walk past this particular church, you would think it was a store. It is located on the main drag in town near the bars, restaurants, and shops. Behind the church, and directly behind my booth, was the church's parking lot. Only it was not just the church parking lot. They also called their parking lot "courthouse" parking so that they could charge people going to the courts a parking fee. The church parking lot was not really competition for parking patrons, as it was much smaller and resembled something out of the 1950s. When an attendant was not on duty, parkers had to insert their money into a metal cash box marked with numbered slots, each corresponding to the parking spot numbers in the parking lot. This created a ton of confusion because people did not get a receipt or ticket for their vehicle to prove that they paid, some did not have exact change to put in the box, and some just did not understand this system of payment. So when the church parking lot was not staffed, which was every day after 1:45 pm, people who had parked there would venture across the street to me with a thousand questions about the parking procedures for the church parking lot. I would encourage them to move over to my parking lot and save themselves the confusion. Some, noticing that the church lot operated on an honor system, and that nobody was watching, would just park and not pay. This hurt the afternoon business in the parking lot where I worked because it gave a free haven for parking with no repercussions.

Each day from 7:45 am-1:45 pm the church parking lot was staffed. Like the lot where I worked, they too had only one employee. Their employee was a man in his late 50s, perhaps early 60s. Let's call him Moe. Moe was quite a character. He wore jeans that looked like they were from the acid wash era, a Home Depot apron tied around his waist, and a Member's Only style jacket. He also wore a hat that made him look like a dead ringer for the killer in "I Know What You Did Last Summer." All he needed was the hook. Moe would show up at exactly 7:47 am each day and perform a very regimented routine which included putting out his five-dollar parking signs, sweeping his parking lot, and filling up his Gatorade cooler with water. After his routine was complete, he would stand on the corner and try to lure cars into his parking lot. Moe's strategy was to point at each car that passed by with the index finger on his left hand, while wiggling the pointer finger on his right hand as if he was trying to lure a kid into a van with candy. This creeped out a lot of people, especially female customers. I would get dozens of comments from people who parked at my lot that were something along the lines of "What's up with that guy across the street? He creeps me out!"

Moe and I had a few run-ins over the course of the more than two years that I worked at the parking lot. He did not like my aggressive New York approach to business, my language, and my criticism of him. On many occasions, I vented my frustration about the lack of afternoon and weekend event staffing at the church parking lot, which would result in me having to handle all of the questions, requests for change, and confusion that went along with his unstaffed lot. Moe was a slow talking, simple minded kind of guy, so my personality and his did not mesh all that well. He most likely threw a party after I left the job, and I don't blame him.

After my first few run-ins with Moe, I would do subtle shit to mess with him. I arrived at work each morning about ninety minutes before Moe, so I had time to come up with ways to annoy him without him knowing I was the source of his annoyance. For example, I would bring stale, crushed bread from home and scatter it all over the church parking lot under the cover of the 6:00 am darkness. By the time he came to work, there were hundreds of pigeons and other birds all over his parking lot. He would dance around flying, shitting birds for hours. With all of the litter in both of the parking lots each morning, combined with the fact that he was simple minded, Moe never realized I was the one putting all of the bread in his lot. It was truly fun to watch.

One particular morning, not too long before I quit, I came across a few dozen snack packs of those orange crackers with the peanut butter between them. I had purchased a bulk pack of them from Costco and brought them to work to have as a snack. But, I never ate them all, and now they were expired. I decided to toss the few dozen packs of crackers into Moe's parking lot and let the birds, squirrels, and the rest of the county's wildlife have at it. Some of the packs broke open because of the impact of the forty foot throw across the street into Moe's parking lot, but some packs stayed intact. When Moe arrived at his normal 7:47 am, he walked the lot and gathered all the packs that survived the throw and placed them in his little shack. After his morning routine, Moe was performing his creepy car pointing ritual while eating the expired parking lot crackers! My goodbye gift to Moe, he just didn't know it.

The church was also known for hiring people off the street. Literally, off the street. They would round up shady people off the street to do weeding and other outdoor maintenance work in or around their parking lot. They would "pay" these characters with a meal, not with money. On hot days, I would bring these temporary workers cold drinks because I kind of felt bad for them. They'd be working all day out in the heat with nothing to drink. Some of these "workers" were a bit unstable, mentally. I found this out after interactions with some them. One day after bringing one of their workers some cold drinks, he tossed the empty beverage bottles across the street into my parking lot. When I went outside to ask why he threw the empties into my parking lot, he went on some incoherent rant about God, a fish dinner, and The Wizard of Oz.

One summer day, there was a knock on my booth door. When I opened it, there stood one of the hired street workers from the church. I asked the disheveled man standing at my door what I could help him with. He asked to borrow my broom with the standing dustpan tray. Against my better judgment, I lent him my cleaning ensemble, instructing him to please bring it back when he was done. I knew if he did not bring it back, I would not have anything to use to clean my parking lot, which needed cleaning more than I care to remember. So a few hours went by and I noticed the worker just sitting on the curb.

ME: *Yelling across the street.* Hey, are you done with my broom and pan? Can I have it back?

BIZARRE BROOM BORROWER: Ain't done yet man! Just takin' a break!

ME: Ok, don't forget to return it!

BIZARRE BROOM BORROWER: I'll try to remember!

An hour or so went by and Bizarre Broom Borrower was still sitting there on the curb, my broom and tray nowhere in sight. My parking lot had trash starting to accumulate from the pigs that parked there all day, so I really wanted the thing back. But I figured, why nag this not so stable guy? Let him finish and I'll get it back before I leave for the day. A few minutes later, two Sheriff's cars pulled up by the church parking lot. The deputies got out of the cars and started talking to the Bizarre Broom Borrower. Within a few seconds, Bizarre Broom Borrower was screaming while the officers cuffed him. Curious about the status of my broom set, I ventured over to the scene of the action.

ME: Hey guys, how's it going?

OFFICER #1: Who are you?

ME: I own the broom he borrowed, just want it back.

BIZARRE BROOM BORROWER: *On the ground screaming.* I didn't do nothing! I didn't do nothing!

ME: *Motioning to Bizarre Broom Borrower.* Excuse me, where's my broom?

BIZARRE BROOM BORROWER: *Screaming.* HEEEEEEEELP! I DIDN'T DO NOTHING!

ME: Ummmm, do you have my broom and tray? Where did you put it?

OFFICER #2: What do you want?

ME: Just trying to find out where my broom is, that's all. Oh and the tray that goes with it, it's a set.

OFFICER #2: Do you think this is an appropriate time to discuss a broom?

ME: Well, you see officer, if you take him away, I won't know where the broom set is. Can you ask him about the broom?

OFFICER #1: *Looking at Bizarre Broom Borrower, annoyed.* Do you have his broom?

BIZARRE BROOM BORROWER: *Screaming.* I DIDN'T DO NOTHING! I DIDN'T STEAL A BROOM!

OFFICER #2: You're going to have to forget the broom!

ME: Unbelievable, now I'm out a broom! How am I going to clean now?!

So I walked away, back to my booth across the street. A few minutes later, the officers managed to get Bizarre Broom Borrower on his feet and were calmly talking to him next to one of the Sheriff's cars. He seemed to have settled down quite a bit. This would be the perfect time to ask about the broom! I opened my booth door and yelled.

ME: Hey! (*all three now looked my way*) Any word on the broom?

OFFICER #1: Do you think we're over here discussing a broom?

ME: Just asking! Figured he was calm now and would remember where he stashed it!

The two officers just shook their heads in amazement that I continued to press on about the status of the broom. They placed the still cuffed, Bizarre Broom Borrower into one of the Sheriff's vehicles and drove away. I had the sneaking suspicion that I was officially out a broom and tray. I walked over to the church parking lot to search for the broom and tray, but it never resurfaced. I went to Wal-Mart the next day to purchase a new

A WHOLE LOT OF SHENANIGANS

cleaning set. The whereabouts of the original broom and tray set remains a mystery.

The church held Bible study classes every Tuesday morning. For a long while, Moe would place signs in his parking lot that read "Church Parking Only" on those Tuesdays so that he would have plenty of parking available for the women and children that came each week for the Bible study class. At some point, he stopped reserving spaces for the church members and they would end up in my parking lot, assuming that they did not have to pay because they were there for church. After informing each person that they had to pay, they would yell at me, as if it were my fault that Moe did not save them a spot. This was another bone of contention that I had with Moe. On one extremely rainy, off-the-charts busy Tuesday Morning, a young lady approached my payment window.

CHILD CARE CUSSER: Goddamn it, it is fucking busy here today!

ME: Indeed, it is! Traffic court, foreclosure auction, Bible study across the street, you name it!

CHILD CARE CUSSER: You think they'd all coordinate their fuckin' schedules!

ME: Agreed. It is chaos here!

CHILD CARE CUSSER: I'm glad you mentioned Bible study, I am one of the child care teachers there today. They told me I could just park here for free.

ME: No ma'am, that free church parking is across the street over by that guy with the hat on. That's the church parking lot.

CHILD CARE CUSSER: There were no fucking spots over there!

133

ME: Well, you are welcome to park here, but you have to pay. We are not affiliated with the church.

CHILD CARE CUSSER: *Pointing up at Moe's sign that also read "Courthouse Parking."* But aren't you the same name? Both lots have the same goddamn name!

ME: They do ma'am, but without giving you a complete history lesson, I'll just say, they took the same name as us years ago so they could charge the public for parking also.

CHILD CARE CUSSER: What fucking good does all this do me? I am here now!

ME: Well if you don't want to pay, I suggest you walk over to that guy Moe and ask him for the five dollars to subsidize your parking so you can pay me, since he did not reserve enough parking for all of you today.

CHILD CARE CUSSER: *Yelling.* FUUUUUUUUUCK ME! I don't have time for this bullshit today! I have to be inside in, like, 4 minutes!

ME: I am sorry ma'am but we have nothing to do with that church.

CHILD CARE CUSSER: I'll just go to my car and get the fucking money! How much is it?

ME: Five dollars.

CHILD CARE CUSSER: I'll be right back, now I am gonna get fuckin' soaked again!

Child Care Cusser retrieved her five-dollar bill and ran off to teach the sweet, innocent children of the church all about the Bible. I would have loved to have been a fly on the wall for that morning's toddler Bible class:

CHILD CARE CUSSER: Ok kids, take your goddamn seats and take out your fuckin' Bibles! Ok, so in the beginning God created

Heaven and the fuckin' earth! The earth was without form, and so fuckin' void, and darkness was upon the face of the deep! God then yelled "Let there be light!" and there was so much fuckin' light!........hey Johnny, pay attention you little bastard!

That storefront church was quite the interesting place, chock full o' colorful characters, creepy parking attendants, profane professors, and the occasional broom thief. Bless their hearts.

Smoked Out!

No single issue caused more altercations at the parking lot than the no smoking policy I had at the payment window. I did not care if people smoked by their cars, or while they walked to or from the parking lot, I just did not want them smoking at the window. The open payment window created a vacuum of sorts, which sucked the cigarette smoke from outside into the booth. That, combined with the inordinate amount of smokers that came to court, was a recipe for lung cancer. Without exaggeration, I dealt with well over 50 smokers per day. I even encountered a chain smoker wearing a "Whoever Said Winning Was Easy Never Had to Battle Lung Cancer" t-shirt. I shit you not.

To enforce the no smoking policy at the payment window, I mounted five, yes five, "No Smoking" signs all over the booth. These signs were large enough so that someone 50 feet away from the booth could read them and extinguish their cigarette well in advance of approaching the window. I also had signs all around the actual payment window itself, ensuring that if someone could see me, they could clearly see a no smoking sign. These signs not only said "NO SMOKING" but had a picture of a cigarette in the big red circle, with the red line through it, you know the one, the international symbol for NO. Do you think almost a half dozen, large no smoking signs prevented people from smoking at the window, right in my face? If you guessed no, you're a winner.

People not only came up smoking, they'd hand me the money with the same hand the lit cigarette was in, actually reaching INSIDE the frame of the window with the lit cigarette itself. They would talk to me with the lit cigarette hanging from their lips as the smoke engulfed my entire face. They would blow the smoke right at me as if that were just normal. After a month of going home daily with headaches, enough was enough. I cracked down and strictly enforced the no smoking policy, which lead to all out steel cage matches of death with some inconsiderate, and quite possibly illiterate smokers. Most smoking encounters were resolved rather peacefully where the violator would apologize and put the cigarette out. Other encounters would lead to some obnoxious barbs being fired back and forth where the cigarette may or may not have been extinguished. Then there were the knock 'em down, drag 'em out fights started by those who loved smoking so much, they would not take no smoking for an answer.

ME: Good Morning Sir!

CHEMTRAIL CHRIS: *Puffing away on a cigarette.* Hello, I need to pay for spot 16.

ME: I am sorry sir, there is no smoking at the window, don't you see the signs?

CHEMTRAIL CHRIS: Give me a fucking break, I am outside!

ME: You may be outside sir, but your smoke comes in here through the window.

CHEMTRAIL CHRIS: How's that my problem?

ME: It's your problem because you're the one creating the fuckin' smoke. If you don't put it out, I'll have to ask you to leave.

CHEMTRAIL CHRIS: *Angrily stomping out his cigarette.* Boy the media has fuckin' sheep like you brainwashed!

ME: What does the media have to do with you being an asshole and not following the posted rules?

CHEMTRAIL CHRIS: The government and media have you believing cigarette smoke is bad for you! You're a fucking sheep!

ME: Sir, it is way too early in the day to debate decades of scientific research and studies with you, and you probably would not comprehend them anyway.

CHEMTRAIL CHRIS: I know plenty about science! You're sitting here worried about my cigarette and they're spraying chemtrails all over us! Keep listening to the "lamestream" media bro!

ME: Sir, chemtrails are a made up conspiracy theory, what comes out of planes are condensation trails made up of ice crystals.

CHEMTRAIL CHRIS: Bullshit! Cancer agents, population control, that's what's coming out of those planes! Just like the *(making air quotes with his nicotine stained fingers)* "fluoride" in the water! They are controlling us and you worry about my cigarette! So ignorant!

ME: I'll tell you what, you take your chances with smoking and I'll take mine without smoking, ok?

CHEMTRAIL CHRIS: They got your mind bro! The government and media got your mind!

ME: Ok sir, we are done here. I hope you have a good day and I really hope they allow you in the courthouse today!

CHEMTRAIL CHRIS: Why wouldn't they let me in, because of what I believe in? Because I speak the fuckin' truth?

ME: No sir, they may not allow you in when the alarm on the metal detector goes crazy because of the tin foil hat you have on. You may want to leave it in your car.

CHEMTRAIL CHRIS: Fuck you sheep! BAAAA! BAAAA! *(doing his best sheep impersonation as he walked away).*

As Chemtrail Chris walked away I knew he would get what was coming to him someday. Somewhere on this big, flat earth, probably at a FEMA concentration camp, the Illuminati would track him down. They'd put him on the mother ship, with Elvis, Kurt Cobain, and Jim Morrison, and send them all to the moon, a place no other man has been before.

A few weeks later, I had another interesting encounter with a defiant smoker.

ME: Good morning sir, before I help you can you put out your cigarette? There are signs all over here that say no smoking.

SMOKIN' STEVE: I can't read.

ME: Ok, be that as it may, now I'm verbally telling you to put out the cigarette.

SMOKIN' STEVE: You discriminating against people who don't read none?

ME: Sir, how am I discriminating against you? I asked you politely to put out the cigarette, it is in violation of our rules.

SMOKIN' STEVE: Yeah, but I can't read!

ME: Sir, even if you can't read, I verbally instructed you to put the cigarette out and two of the signs show a cigarette with a line through it, you don't have to know how to read to understand that picture.

SMOKIN' STEVE: Fuck you, I will park someplace else!

ME: Ok, have a great day sir!

Smokin' Steve then proceeded to give me the finger with BOTH hands!

ME: *Yelling.* I am sorry sir, I can't read sign language!

These fine folks were not taking kindly to the no smoking at the payment window policy. But the best smoking story came on a busy Autumn afternoon. A huge overall wearing, chain-smoking man was walking toward the booth oblivious to the multiple, huge no smoking signs.

ME: Sir, there is no smoking here at the window, if you'd like to finish your cigarette over by your car, that's fine, otherwise you'll have to put it out.

MARLBORO MIKE: *Dropped the cigarette, put it out, and blew the smoke of his last drag right in my face.* How much for parking?

ME: Did you just blow that smoke in my face?

MARLBORO MIKE: *Laughing.* You said no cigarette at the window, you said nothing about blowing the smoke!

ME: You're a complete asshole.

MARLBORO MIKE: Yeah, but I ain't the asshole with smoke in my face!

ME: *Ready to kill this guy.* It's five dollars to park, cash or card?

MARLBORO MIKE: *Hands me a five-dollar bill.* Cash.

I did not say thank you or anything else, and I just let him walk away because I was livid and would have beaten the crap out of this guy if I were outside. A few hours later, around noon, Marlboro Mike drove off out of the parking lot. One less asshole, I thought to myself. About 1:15 pm, I saw Marlboro Mike pull back into the lot and park again. He was headed back to court for the afternoon session. Apparently Marlboro Mike didn't bother to read our "No In & Out Privileges" sign right next to the "No Smoking" sign because Marlboro Mike started to walk back to court without paying for his second parking space.

ME: *Yelling.* Excuse Me! You cannot go in and out without paying again!

MARLBORO MIKE: What's this you say?

ME: If you leave the parking lot and reenter, you have to pay again.

MARLBORO MIKE: All I did was go to lunch!

ME: Sorry sir, like the no smoking, those are the rules!

MARLBORO MIKE: *Reaching for his pack of cigarettes and laughing like he told the joke of a lifetime.* Want a smoke?

ME: No sir, if I wanted a good laugh, I'd ask you to drop your pants.

MARLBORO MIKE: Yeah, what if I refuse to pay again? I got my ticket from this morning, how you gonna prove what time I paid?

ME: I guess don't pay again and you'll find out.

So Marlboro Mike, feeling he had to win a pissing contest after my small penis insinuation, walked away without paying for his reentry. I immediately called our fly by night towing service. It just so happened that they had a truck in the area when I called. Twenty minutes later, Marlboro Mike's vehicle was on the flatbed and on its way to the impound yard a few miles away. Around 2:30 pm, Marlboro Mike came out of court, and moseyed on back to the parking lot as he smoked yet another cigarette. As he got closer to where his car should have been, he realized he made a big mistake in fucking with me:

MARLBORO MIKE: Where the fuck is my car?

ME: I told you the rules and you were an asshole.

MARLBORO MIKE: Where's my fucking car!?

ME: It is at the impound yard. Instead of paying five dollars, now it is 175 dollars. The number to the tow company is posted right next to the no smoking and no in and out signs.

MARLBORO MIKE: You haven't heard the end of this!

Marlboro Mike then phoned the impound yard to determine what he needed to do to get his ashtray on wheels back. He waited around for a few more minutes until a car arrived to pick him up to take him to the impound yard. As he opened the passenger's door to get in his chauffeured ride, I yelled "Hey!" Marlboro Mike looked over and I yelled "Now go home and get your fuckin' shine box!"

Marlboro Mike got his comeuppance, I got my revenge, but most of all I got to use a line from the movie Goodfellas I'd been dying to use for decades. Later, at the end of my workday, some of the neighborhood kids carried my lunch cooler and laptop bag all the way to my car. You know why? It was outta respect!

Prejudiced Pups?

The amount of parking customers who made the decision to bring their dogs with them when they were headed into court was astounding to me. As a dog lover and owner, it simply would not occur to me to bring any of my dogs to a place where I could not bring them inside or where I had no idea how long I was going to be inside. But like everything else, in the parking lot, logic and common sense were rarely factors in the decision making process of the customers.

Many of the people who made the foolish decision to bring their dogs with them to court would let me know they had a dog in their car, where they were parked and that their windows were open, water was available to the dog and things of that nature. While I was not a proponent of leaving a dog in a car, I was appreciative that they let me know, so I could at least check up on the precious pups from time to time. Most dogs left in cars were calm and simply went to sleep until their owners returned from court. Some barked for a while then settled down. Others barked incessantly until their owners returned. It was a mixed bag of canine behaviors.

There were also people who chose to bring their dogs to court that would not let me know that their dog was being left in their car while they were inside handling their affairs. In many instances, I would be made aware that a dog was in a car by a concerned person who parked next the car with a dog inside. In those instances, I would head out and check on the dog to ensure it was safe, had air, water, etc. On other occasions, if a car with a dog inside was parked close enough to my booth, I would hear barking and head out to investigate.

On one busy late June morning, a man who was visibly upset approached the payment window to pay for his parking:

ME: Good Morning Sir, how are you today?

OFFENDED OSCAR: Man, that's some racist bullshit right down there!

ME: I'm sorry sir, what happened, what's racist?

OFFENDED OSCAR: That's as racist as it gets!

ME: Sir, did someone yell a slur at you? What happened?

OFFENDED OSCAR: Them fuckin' dogs!

ME: What dogs, sir? I'm a bit confused.

OFFENDED OSCAR: You got some racist-ass dogs up in this bitch!

ME: Racist dogs? Were you chased by dogs?

OFFENDED OSCAR: I am parked down up along the road on the side, spot 19!

ME: Ok, spot 19, did something happen there?

OFFENDED OSCAR: Look at them racist pieces of shit in spot 20, in that minivan!

ME: *Squinting.* Is someone in there, sir?

OFFENDED OSCAR: No but them racist ass dogs are in there!

ME: There are dogs in the minivan and they're racists?

OFFENDED OSCAR: Fuck yeah! I was sittin' up in my car eatin' breakfast and every time a black person walked by they were growling and barking, but when a white person went by.... NOTHIN'!

ME: That's very odd sir.

OFFENDED OSCAR: Then soon as I got out the motherfuckin' car they went crazy! Then white people passed, nothing!

ME: *Not knowing what to say*. Very, very strange.

OFFENDED OSCAR: That ain't strange! Them bitches be trained for that shit!

ME: I'll take your word for it sir, you seemed to have been sitting there quite a while observing.

OFFENDED OSCAR: Damn straight!

Offended Oscar paid for his parking and started to walk away towards the courthouses. Then he decided to do an about face and headed towards the minivan full of allegedly racist dogs. Offended Oscar pulled out his smartphone and recorded the dogs barking at him while he narrated his story. While still recording, he walked a few cars down and ducked, so that the allegedly racist dogs could no longer see him. The dogs stopped barking. Offended Oscar kept filming until a white person passed the minivan, and...not a peep from the biased barkers as a white lady passed by the minivan! Offended Oscar may have been onto something!

OFFENDED OSCAR: You see that shit?!

ME: I did see it!

OFFENDED OSCAR: I got that shit on tape! Shit's going on YouTube and Facebook! Shit's gonna go viral!

ME: If I did not see it, I probably would not have believed it, sir!

OFFENDED OSCAR: That's why I filmed that bitch, nobody woulda believed me!

Offended Oscar went on his merry way while looking down at his phone. He was probably starting to post his mini-documentary on social media. While slightly convinced, I still was a tad unsure if Offended Oscar had a large enough sample size to be able to fully claim that those dogs were, indeed, full blown racists.

Once the morning rush was complete and things slowed down a bit, I strolled over to the minivan to do my own investigation. I remembered seeing an episode of "Curb Your Enthusiasm" that featured a racist dog, but I assumed it was merely a comedy sketch that could not possibly be true. As I approached the minivan, three dogs were looking out the back window, excited to see me, but not barking. They were just jumping around and wagging their tails. Ok, they didn't bark at me, a white guy, so Offended Oscar's theory still held true. But I had to finish my investigation. A few minutes later, a court reporter who parked in the lot each day arrived. Sheila just so happened to be African American, so perhaps she'd help me with my study:

SHEILA: Good Morning Charlie!

ME: Hey Sheila, how's it going today?

SHEILA: Thought today was Friday when I woke up, disappointed to discover it is only Thursday!

ME: I hear you, it's been a long week!

Sheila paid for her parking and started to gather her stuff for court.

ME: Sheila, can I ask a favor?

SHEILA: Of course!

ME: There was a guy here earlier who was a bit disturbed by something. I don't want to give you the details until we look into it together. Do you have like two minutes?

SHEILA: For you, of course!

ME: Take a walk with me, it's right over there *(pointing to the minivan).*

SHEILA: That van?

ME: Yeah. I am going to stop here, can you walk over towards the van?

SHEILA: *Nervously laughing.* What's at the van?

ME: Nothing that will hurt you, I just want to see something!

SHEILA: Ok, I am trusting you Charlie!

Sheila cautiously walked towards the minivan. As she got about ten feet or so from it, the dogs went wild barking! Sheila, got a bit startled and walked quickly back towards me.

SHEILA: Did you want me to look at those crazy dogs?

ME: No, I wanted them to see you!

SHEILA: I'm not sure I get it!

I went on to explain all that transpired with Offended Oscar, his video, and my independent study. Sheila, who was normally amused by my daily anecdotes and parking lot tales, laughed until she had tears in her eyes.

SHEILA: Leave it to you Charlie! I have to tell my husband about this one! He loves the stories from here!

ME: You are the best Sheila! Thanks so much! Have a great day, see you tomorrow!

SHEILA: Yes, you will...and tomorrow WILL be Friday!

So there it was. Offended Oscar's detailed observations while he ate breakfast, his interaction with the pups, his video, and my study. It was official, we indeed did have some racist motherfuckin' dogs in the lot! The only thing left was to see who the owners were.

Around noon, people started filing out of court for the afternoon recess. I was eager to see who owned these dogs! I started taking bets in my mind as to who the owner was going to be. Then, my eyes locked in on a man wearing a t-shirt with a confederate flag on the front of it, was this him? He passed by the booth, and I noticed that the back of his shirt said "The Fourth means Family, Faith, Fireworks, and Firearms!" He headed in the direction of the minivan, but then passed it right by and got into his pickup truck. Not a peep from the pups! While my eyes were on him, an African-American family of five walked past my booth and straight towards the minivan. The dogs went wild again! I thought to myself, Offended Oscar was spot on! The family then pressed their key fob to deactivate the alarm on the minivan and got in, to the delight of the three pups. The dogs jumped on the kids, kissed them, and were just so happy to see them all! I stood there dumbfounded. Those dogs had us all fooled! As funny as I thought the story was, it was a learning lesson. Things aren't always what they appear to be, even with a little bit of amateur investigation by Offended Oscar and me. At least one courthouse story had a happy ending. No racist pups here!

Waste Mismanagement

Nothing really annoys me more in my everyday travels than people who litter. I see it everywhere. I see it in parking lots, on highways, in parks, and in other public places. I just do not understand the act of littering. How difficult is it to place something you no longer need into a nearby trash can, or if no trash can is immediately available, hold on to that item until you find one? What do litterers think happens to the trash they leave behind? Do they even think about it, or is it a "no longer my problem" kind of an attitude?

Dealing with trash was an all day, everyday struggle at the parking lot. For starters, we did not offer the customers a place to throw away their trash. Yeah, you read that right, we were a business with no trash can. Well, I did have a tiny sized trash can in the booth for small things that I needed to throw away, but nothing for the thousand or so people who parked at the lot each week. After less than a week at the job, I immediately realized this was a problem and had a conversation with the owners about it.

ME: I think we need a trash can out in the lot. There is trash all over the lot each day and it is difficult to keep up with.

OWNER: People are going to litter whether there's a trash can out there or not.

ME: But, why not give them the opportunity to throw it away? Plus, I'll have a place to throw away the trash that does end up in the lot instead of lugging it across the street and down the block to the dumpster every morning.

OWNER: Well, it will smell in the warm weather, and the flies.

ME: But I am the only one that's here that will have to deal with flies and stink. Plus, if we get a can on wheels with an attached lid, it won't smell, there will be no flies, and I can just wheel it down the block when it's full and empty it.

OWNER: Yeah but kids will come at night and tip it over or steal it.

ME: Why don't we just chain it to the pole in the back of the booth with a padlock? This way they can't tip it or take it?

OWNER: I'll look into it.

Well, like with many other issues, the owners never looked into it. I'd mention it at least one or twice a month and I'd just get the rubbish runaround. Not having a garbage can created problems for those who actually wanted to do the right thing and throw away their trash. On a daily basis, I'd have people come up to the booth to pay for their parking with empty coffee cups, banana peels, fast food bags, and a host of other items only to explain to them that the closest garbage pail was across the street. This didn't sit well with most and they'd ask if I had a pail inside the booth. I would explain to them that I just had a small office pail and that it didn't hold much. Most people ended up trekking their trash over to the courts, but a lot of it ended up on the ground in the parking lot.

Each morning, under the cover of darkness, I would arrive at a trash covered parking lot just raring to go! Rain or snow, heat or cold, I'd grab my broom along with my oversized standing dustpan and head outside to clean up. I'd be greeted by dirty diapers, cigarette butts, fast food bags, bottles and cans, auto parts, used feminine hygiene products, toothbrushes, dental picks, clothing, beer cups from the late night patrons at the local pub, spent fireworks, vomit, and pretty much every other vile excretion and item you can think of. I even found an oil pan full of oil, apparently left by someone who decided to perform an overnight oil change in the parking lot. On a good morning, it would take me fifteen minutes to get the lot cleaned, on a bad morning upwards of forty-five minutes. So by 7:00 am, nobody would ever know that the now spotless lot looked like a garbage barge just thirty minutes prior. It was always clean and ready for the first customers to arrive.

It did not take long for the trash in the lot to accumulate. Some customers ate breakfast in their cars and decided the ground was a good place to dispose of their cups and bags. By 9:30 am on any given morning, the parking lot was full of trash once again. I would do my best to try to catch and publically shame anyone littering. One morning, I watched as a group of young men tossed water bottles, wrappers, and a fast food bag onto the ground. They then walked up to the payment window to pay for their parking.

ME: Good Morning Guys.

LITTERING LAMAR: What's up man? How much for the parking?

ME: Five dollars sir, are you using cash or card?

LITTERING LAMAR: Cash all day bro, here you go.

ME: Thank you. Can I ask you something?

LITTERING LAMAR: Ugh, yeah.

ME: What did you throw on the ground down there?

A look of shock came over Littering Lamar's face as his friends taunted him by saying "Oh Shit! Oh Shit! He called your ass out!"

LITTERING LAMAR: Ugh, it was a couple of water bottles, some candy wrappers, and a Chik-Fil-A bag.

ME: Can I ask why you'd do that?

LITTERING LAMAR: I don't know, to be honest.

Littering Lamar's friends then really started getting on him. "You are stone cold busted! He got you! Oh Shit!"

LITTERING LAMAR: *Laughing to his friends*. This guy has got some balls callin' me out on that shit, don't he? Man, you got me!

ME: I wasn't trying to embarrass you, but we just try to keep the parking lot and the town nice for everyone. I just didn't understand why you did it and wanted to ask.

LITTERING LAMAR: No man, you're good, you got balls, I respect that! You know what I'm going to do?

ME: What's that?

LITTERING LAMAR: I'm going to go down there and pick that shit up, that's what I'm going to do! Pick it up 'cause you got balls and because you are right, I shouldn't have done it!

Littering Lamar shook my hand and I thanked him in advance for relocating his refuse to a garbage pail down by the bus stop. Littering Lamar and his pals laughed all the way to the pail and beyond. Not everyone was as cordial and receptive to being called out for littering, like the mother of a woman who approached the payment window on a hot summer morning.

CONVERTIBLE CAROL: Just so you know, my two kids and my mom are going to stay in the car while I go into court.

ME: Ok, that's fine ma'am.

152

CONVERTIBLE CAROL: It's that convertible over there. They are going to have breakfast and wait for me. My mom is watching them.

ME: Sure, no problem.

Convertible Carol walked over to court while her mother and children sat in the convertible and ate breakfast. A few minutes later, I noticed an array of fast food bags, cups, and wrappers surrounding the convertible. I approached the vehicle and asked a few questions.

ME: Hey everyone, good morning.

BACKSEAT BILLY: Hi!

ME: Is this your trash outside the car?

GRUMPY GRANNY: Ain't ours!

ME: I am pretty sure it is. The lot was cleaned an hour ago, you all were eating out of bags, now all the bags and trash are on the ground. Nobody else was here.

GRUMPY GRANNY: I said, it ain't ours!

BACKSEAT BILLY: But nana you....

GRUMPY GRANNY: Shut up Billy, it ain't ours!

ME: Go ahead Billy, say what you were going to say.

GRUMP GRANNY: Don't you talk to him, get out of here!

BACKSEAT BONNIE: Nana, you told us to...

GRUMPY GRANNY: What did I tell you, shut up!

ME: No problem kids, I understand.

I proceeded to get a trash bag from my booth and I picked up all the trash and placed it into the bag as Grumpy Granny watched. There was so much trash that it filled half of the white kitchen sized trash bag. Grumpy Granny thought she had won. But Grumpy Granny did not know who she was fucking with. Kids or no kids, she was going to learn a lesson, and perhaps the kids would as well.

Convertible Carol came out of court about forty-five minutes later. I stopped her to inform her that her mom was setting a bad example for her kids by telling them to litter the ground and then lie about it. Convertible Carol said she would talk to her Mom about it and thanked me for letting her know. She then asked me how to get back to the interstate. I purposely directed her on a route that would force her to go on the road behind my booth where there was an intersection and a traffic light. Convertible Carol eased out of the lot and slowly took the route I had given her. When they stopped for the traffic light, I ran outside and up to Grumpy Granny's side of the car with the bagful of trash she had dumped. I yelled "Grandma, give a hoot, don't pollute!" and dumped all of her trash in her lap. The kids in the backseat, along with Carol the driver, screamed with laughter as a shocked Grumpy Granny stared me down with a stunned look on her face. I ran back towards my booth feeling the thrill of victory.

The kids probably had no idea who the fuck Woodsy Owl was, or what giving a hoot meant, but at least they got a good laugh and a life lesson out of my garbage gag on their Grumpy Granny.

Outhouse, In the Middle of Our Street

People expected quite a lot of service with their five-dollar parking fee. They assumed I would watch their pets, tend to their children, fix their cars, and offer them a host of other non-parking related goods and services all for one low, flat rate. One of the most frequent requests was for use of a restroom. A restroom I didn't have. I was locked up in an 8' x 8' wooden shack all day. The shack resembled the type of shed you would see for sale at Home Depot, one of those really expensive sheds with a couple of windows and a door. But a shack nonetheless. That did not stop the general public from assuming that I had a full restroom inside my wooden cell. Little did they know that my restroom was two and a half football fields away, in an office building down the block where the owners rented a small office where they kept supplies, traffic cones, signage, and other parking business related items. I barely ever got use of the restroom because by the time I closed the window, put up a "be back in 5 minutes" sign, locked up the cash, locked up the shack, and headed out the door, there would be three people in my face wanting to pay for their parking. So I had to get creative when it came to ways to relieve myself.

My first strategy was not to drink coffee in the morning, because caffeine makes me piss like a thoroughbred. I also limited my intake of any other liquids. But as the summer months here in the South approached, I had to stay hydrated. Of course, with drinking came the natural need to relieve myself. My first thought was to use a jar of some sort. After all, a pickle jar had a large opening on top, held quite a bit of liquid, and I could close it up to prevent spillage inside the shack. But where was I going

155

to empty this? I didn't want to be carrying a urine filled pickle jar that needed emptying down the block with me each day after my shift ended. I also did not want to just dump a jar of urine into the street like I was living in some third world country without indoor plumbing. I guess if it were very rainy out, nobody would have noticed, but it just did not feel right. I needed something more efficient, more discreet, and somewhat sanitary.

When in need, always check Amazon! My wife found bags called "Travel Johns" that people use for camping, long car rides, and so forth. They are tall, narrow bags with an opening on top, that contain a substance inside that turns to gel when mixed with liquid. The bags hold up to twenty-four ounces. So pissing in a bag of gel became the norm for me for almost two years. But before whipping it out to pee, I had to be sure nobody was approaching the shack that could look inside and see me in my luxurious restroom. It was quite a process in an always busy parking lot. In hindsight, after witnessing the guy pissing in the funnel and water balloon for his friend's drug test, I should have sold clean, drug free urine right out of my shack. I could have made a killing.

While I was peeing in bags inside the shack, people were pissing all over, outside the shack. The courts that most customers were headed to were a mere 100 yards across the street, yet people felt compelled to piss, or attempt to piss, right in the parking lot. After a few months of working at the lot, I noticed a very common trait with those that needed to use a restroom, they held or grabbed their crotch area like a child doing the pee-pee dance. Grown adults, male and female, grabbing their crotches to emphasize just how badly they had to go, as if asking for a restroom or letting me know they had to go was not quite enough. I once had a grown man get out of his car and announce to the entire city, "the turtle head is peeking out, the turtle head is peeking out, I gotta shit!" in the middle of the crowded parking lot. If grabbing crotches and turtle head announcements were the worst of it, it would not have been all that bad. But it got worse, a lot worse. One very early morning around 6:20 am a pickup truck pulled into the lot and parked, then an older gentleman exited the vehicle and walked up to the payment window.

ME: Good morning sir, you're here early!

TIM THE TROTTING TINKLER: *Grabbing his crotch.* Oh man, I had a long ride! Any restroom in there?

ME: No sir, unfortunately I do not have a restroom.

TIM THE TROTTING TINKLER: Where is there a restroom around here? I gotta piss like you wouldn't believe!

ME: Unfortunately, just in the courts which open at 8 and the deli around the corner that opens at 7.

TIM THE TROTTING TINKLER: Ain't gonna work for me, I gotta piss NOW!

Tim the Trotting Tinkler unzipped his pants and took out his penis right there at my window.

ME: Sir, what are you doing?!

TIM THE TROTTING TINKLER: I have to piss!

ME: *Yelling.* SIR! You cannot piss here! If you piss up against my building, I will have to smell your urine all day! It's going to be 92 degrees today, do you know what that is going to smell like?

Tim, the Trotting Tinkler, with his penis sticking out of his pants, started running across the street to the church parking lot while he created a zig zagged piss trail on the pavement from the side of my shack all the way to the church. After emptying his full bladder and pissing quite a bit on the left leg of his pants, he casually zipped up and headed back to my payment window to pay for his parking.

ME: *Holding up a large bottle of hand sanitizer.* Before you touch your money or credit card, here, have some of this!

TIM THE TROTTING TINKLER: Good idea, I made a mess! Do you have any baby wipes in there?

ME: No sir, just hand sanitizer.

TIM THE TROTTING TINKLER: That'll have to do then!

I pumped the hand sanitizer into Tinkling Tim's hand and he proceeded to sanitize his hands. He thanked me for the sanitizer, paid for his parking, and then moseyed over to his pickup truck. He climbed into the back of the pickup truck and looked around for something. He then scooted himself out of the bed of the pickup and reached for a gas powered leaf blower. After a few yanks on the pull cord, the blower started up and he used it to try to dry the urine on his soaked pant leg. After drying the piss off of his pants, Tim the Trotting Tinkler sat in his car and waited for court to open while I prayed that the urine trail on the side of my booth would dry up before the hot sun came out.

Using the parking lot as a restroom was certainly not limited to just men. Women also felt the need to drop their pants in the parking lot rather than making that long cross country hike 100 yards across the street to the courthouse. One morning a woman with her husband and teenage daughter pulled into the parking lot at around 6:45 am.

ME: Good Morning folks, how are you all today?

SQUATTING SUZIE: Doing well! We are early! When do the courts open up?

ME: They open at 8:00 am, ma'am.

SQUATTING SUZIE's SPOUSE: Anything open now around here? My wife needs a restroom.

ME: The deli around the corner opens up at 7:00 am, which is fifteen minutes from now.

SQUATTING SUZIE: Oh, that'll work!

Squatting Suzie paid her five-dollar parking fee and then she, along with her family, got back into their car which was parked about four spaces away from my booth. I had a clear view of the vehicle from my side door. Squatting Suzie's husband got back into the driver's seat, Squatting Suzie into the passenger's seat, and her daughter into the backseat. Everything seemed quiet and normal until a few minutes later when I went over to the door to have a look outside. It was at that moment that I witnessed Squatting Suzie's ass hanging out of the passenger side door. Her knees were up on the passenger's seat and she positioned her ass just so, that it hung ever so slightly outside of the car door frame. Squatting Suzie then proceeded to pee onto the pavement, sending a stream of urine cascading down the lot as the rising sun reflected upon it. Squatting Suzie then stood up outside of the car, narrowly missed stepping into her freshly made stream, as her daughter handed her tissues to wipe herself. Squatting Suzie wiped, then tossed the tissues onto the ground. I opened the booth door and we exchanged pleasantries.

ME: Ma'am it's bad enough that you peed in the lot, but did you have to throw your toilet paper onto the ground?!

SQUATTING SUZIE: It blew out of my hand! And it was a tissue not toilet paper!

ME: Once you wipe your privates with something, it becomes toilet paper, no matter what it started out as!

SQUATTING SUZIE: Well it blew away from my hand! *Just then a small gust of wind took her pee soaked Kleenex and sent it flying across the lot.* See! It's gone!

ME: Disgusting!

SQUATTING SUZIE: Maybe if you people provided a bathroom, people wouldn't have to do this!

ME: When have you ever heard of a parking lot providing a bathroom? The courts do have bathrooms and I explained to you that the deli around the corner was about to open, but you chose to piss in the lot!

SQUATTING SUZIE: Go back inside and mind your own fucking business!

ME: People pissing all over the lot is my business!

Disgusted, I slammed the door and went back inside. Squatting Suzie, however, wasn't done with her morning routine. Now that she was done relieving herself, she proceeded to the back of the vehicle where she opened the trunk. Squatting Suzie, with her daughter now standing next to her, decided to take her t-shirt off. Standing in her bra, she decided to put on some deodorant, and then moved on to her moisturizing regimen as she lathered her skin with cocoa butter. Her daughter helped with those hard to reach areas on her back. Fully moisturized, Squatting Suzie then put on a court appropriate blouse and tossed her previously worn t-shirt into the trunk. Done? I think not! Suzie, with her daughter's assistance, slipped out of her sweatpants and into a more formal skirt. She then applied her makeup as her daughter held a small mirror. Now fully dressed, moisturized, made up, and relieved, Squatting Suzie and her family headed off to the deli around the corner and then on to court.

It was clear that Squatting Suzie did not give a crap about conforming to a civilized society and that her daughter, as a teen, was not expected to be the voice of reason, but what the fuck was wrong with her husband? He sat there silently as his wife's bare ass hung out a car door, as she stood in her bra for ten minutes moisturizing and as she took her sweatpants off and changed into a skirt as cars were passing by. If my wife started to squat out a car door with a parking attendant fifteen feet away and while cars were passing, I would like to think that I would suggest a few alternatives first. But that's just me.

In all fairness to Squatting Suzie and The Trotting Tinkler, even though they did not elect to use it, at least they inquired about a nearby restroom. Some did not even do that. Many people just got out of their cars and just started peeing, no questions asked. I once saw a young guy, through my binoculars, way down in the back of the lot, piss up against the fence while eating an enormous slice of seven-layer chocolate cake. He fed himself the slab of cake with his left hand, while holding his dick with his right. This was in broad daylight, in the middle of the afternoon. All I wanted was for people to act civilized and courteous in the parking lot, pay their fee and go on their way. Oh, and avoid using it as their personal toilet. But, in that parking lot, I could never have my cake and eat it too.

Funny Money

With a fair amount of shady people coming to the parking lot for court on a daily basis, I had to be aware and alert at all times. Even though the police department was down the block and the sheriff's department was across the street, it did not necessarily deter some people from doing illegal shit. People brazenly walked off from the parking lot without paying for their parking, smoked weed, drank, gave urine to their friends for drug tests, littered, fought, tried to vandalize their ex's cars, and engaged in a host of other pleasantries. My concern, since a high percentage of our business was in cash, was being robbed. I was always on alert and prepared for such an incident. Thankfully that never happened.

With a considerable amount of cash tendered each day in combination with shady people, I had to be on alert for counterfeit money. I was pretty good at spotting a phony bill but also had a few of those counterfeit bill pens to double check questionable currency. Some people got creative and cut the corners off twenty dollar bills and glued them to one dollar bills in hopes that you would only look at the corners and not at the entire bill. Having worked retail in my younger years, I knew most of the tricks, so it was difficult to get a phony bill by me. I was most concerned with fifty and one hundred dollar bills. On those bills, we stood to lose the most money, and they were the most commonly counterfeited.

On a late summer morning, a young man approached the payment window with a ten-dollar bill.

ME: Good morning sir, paying for your parking? Which spot number are you in?

COUNTERFEIT CLYDE: Nah, I'm getting on the bus down there at the bus stop. I ain't got nothing smaller than this ten. Can you give me a five and five singles so I can pay for my bus fare?

Giving change to people getting on the bus was a pretty common thing at the parking lot. It is the closest business to the bus stop, so I had people coming up at least once a day for bus fare change.

ME: Sure sir, here you go.

COUNTERFEIT CLYDE: Thanks, man.

ME: You are welcome, have a great day.

Normally, people who requested change for the bus headed right down to the bus stop, which was in plain sight of my booth. But in this instance Counterfeit Clyde headed to a parking lot across the street, where a girl in a car was waiting for him. I immediately realized this guy lied about the bus, and I quickly checked out the ten dollar bill he had given me. I ran the counterfeit pen across the bill and, sure enough, it was a phony. My instincts told me to just let it go. It was ten dollars, I would just put my own money in and throw away the fake. No harm, no foul. I would be out ten, but I would not have to deal with drama. But, that is not how I am wired. It is a genetic, Italian thing where I cannot let someone think they got the best of me or that they made me look like an idiot. It is engrained in me.

I locked up the booth, fake ten-dollar bill in hand, and jogged over to confront Bogus Bonnie and Counterfeit Clyde. Unfortunately, the car they were in was gone. I would not have the opportunity to deliver justice to these two outlaws. But, then it dawned on me that they had to drive around the building where they were parked to exit. I jogged over to the exit, stood there, and waited.

A few seconds later, windows down, radio up, Bogus Bonnie and Counterfeit Clyde came driving around the building in the direction of their only exit and also in the path of a crazy New Yorker holding up their funny money. The look of shock on their faces was priceless.

ME: Hey fucko, nice try. Give me back the ten dollars I gave you.

COUNTERFEIT CLYDE: What are you talkin' about man? I never seen you before in my life!

BOGUS BONNIE: Are you robbing us?

ME: Ask your boyfriend or whatever the fuck he is. He thought he could outhustle me, but look who got hustled.

BOGUS BONNIE: He ain't done nothing! If you don't move I'm calling the police!

COUNTERFEIT CLYDE: Don't know what you are talking about! You fuckin' crazy!

ME: I'll show you just how crazy I am! We can do this the easy way or we can do this the hard way! I have you on camera handing me a counterfeit bill and I have your tag number now. Should I call the police or would you like to?

BOGUS BONNIE: *To Counterfeit Clyde.* Just give it to him, you got warrants.

COUNTERFEIT CLYDE: I ain't giving him shit!

ME: I am not going to wait here all day, are you returning the money or shall I dial the cops?

COUNTERFEIT CLYDE: I guess I'mma give you the money back.

ME: I think that's the smart way to go.

Counterfeit Clyde proceeded to pull a wad of cash out of his pockets and started to hand me the now crumpled and balled up five-dollar bill and five singles.

ME: I don't like what you did to the money, it is all balled up in little balls, I am not accepting that.

COUNTERFEIT CLYDE: What the fuck do you mean? That's the money you gave me!

ME: Yeah, but it was not in little balls! I'm not taking balled up money that you're throwing at me!

COUNTERFEIT CLYDE: Well, that's all I got!

ME: No it's not, I saw that stack you pulled out of your pocket!

COUNTERFEIT CLYDE: That got nothing smaller than a twenty!

ME: That'll do.

COUNTERFEIT CLYDE: What da fuck? You want a twenty for a ten?

ME: That's better than the deal you gave me when I gave you ten for zero over at the window!

COUNTERFEIT CLYDE: *To Bogus Bonnie.* This motherfucker is shaking me down!

ME: That's my offer, take it or leave it!

COUNTERFEIT CLYDE: *Handing me a real, fresh twenty in disbelief.* Here!

ME: Ok, you have a great day, and don't be doing this bullshit to anyone else!

COUNTERFEIT CLYDE: Ain't you going to give me that ten back?

ME: The fake ten?

COUNTERFEIT CLYDE: Yeah, my ten!

ME: No. You're just going to pass it off on another innocent person, it is going in the trash!

COUNTERFEIT CLYDE: So I'mma lose THIRTY dollars now?

ME: No, you lost ten. You gave me the ten back that you stole from me, and you gave me ten for my troubles today, which was the twenty-dollar bill, we are even.

COUNTERFEIT CLYDE: *Confused.* But wait, I gave you twenty, and you have my ten, that's THIRTY!

ME: No sir, you still have my five and five singles, you gave me a twenty...so you are now out ten so you learn your lesson!

COUNTERFEIT CLYDE: But what about the ten-dollar bill?

ME: It's fucking counterfeit, it is worthless, it is fucking paper! Now get out of here before I call the police!

BOGUS BONNIE: *To Counterfeit Clyde.* Let's go!

ME: *As they started rolling away.* Be careful who you try to hustle next time!

When I got back to the booth, I placed the entire twenty into the cash till. That more than replaced the ten that Clyde stole from me. I used the extra ten that I hustled from Counterfeit Clyde to pay for two parking fees for a couple of the regular customers later that afternoon. I figured I may as well do a good deed with the proceeds from my revenge hustle. The fake ten, well that went where it belonged, in the trash with the rest of the worthless paper.

The fun part of encounters like these is that the shady person, in this case Counterfeit Clyde, never saw retribution coming. At most businesses, the guy or girl behind the counter fears for their job, fears a bad online review, or a call to the corporate office and has to stand there and take crap from the public. At this job, I answered to nobody, and truly did not give a shit if I was there the next day or not. After years of taking crap from the public, it was liberating to give it right back to those that deserved it and, in this case, outhustle a hustler.

Thank You for Your Service

The town I worked in was located a few miles from a military reserve base. On Fridays, I would see many of the reservists, in uniform, coming into town for lunch. Many of these ladies and gentlemen parked at the parking lot where I worked, and I got to know them from their weekly visits. We would make small talk with each other, discussing topics such as the weather, where they were headed for lunch, and, on occasion, I would tell them a parking lot story or two to give them a good laugh. They were nice and polite people, and I really respect what they do for the country. I talked to the reservists like I would people in any occupation, and I did not ask about their work unless they brought it up. I also was not over the top with the "thank you for your service." Now, don't get me wrong, I don't think there's anything wrong with thanking a veteran, active service member, or reservist, but I often wonder how sincere some people really are. Do they feel obligated to say it, or are they being genuinely sincere? How do the members of the military feel about it? Is it overkill?

Like clockwork, the reservists started arriving around 11:45 am one Summer Friday. A group of three reservists, two that I knew and one that I did not, arrived together and came up to the window to pay for their parking. We got into some conversation about the upcoming weekend, the Atlanta Braves, and Atlanta Falcons training camp. As we were in mid-conversation, a middle-aged man ran up to the booth and yelled "thank you for your service, oh thank you all! You're all heroes! Oh my God, thank you! Not all heroes wear capes! Oh, thank you! So brave!" The reservist I was talking to rolled his eyes sensing that this guy was not sincere and was just looking for some attention. I held up one finger as if to say wait one minute, watch this.

ME: *To Over the Top Tim*: Hi sir, paying for parking today?

OVER THE TOP TIM: Yes, how much is it?

ME: Five dollars, sir.

OVER THE TOP TIM: Here you go. Can you tell me where traffic court is?

ME: Sure sir, it is the second building on the left.

OVER THE TOP TIM: Great!

ME: You forgetting something?

OVER THE TOP TIM: Ummm...I don't think so!

ME: You didn't thank me for my service!

All of the reservists were now laughing heartily.

OVER THE TOP TIM: *Looking completely bewildered.* Excuse me? Why would I thank you for your service? Are you in the military?

ME: No sir, I am not, but I just rendered a service and gave you directions, I just thought I'd be thanked for my service.

OVER THE TOP TIM: *Angrily.* You didn't risk your life to give me directions! These guys risk their lives!

RESERVIST #1: Sir, we appreciate the gesture, but we just hang on the base, we aren't doing all that much. You should thank this guy for the directions and service he gave you. That was some quality service!

OVER THE TOP TIM: You think so?

RESERVISTS: Definitely!

OVER THE TOP TIM: Ummmm, thank you for the directions.

ME: You really didn't say thank you for your service, but that'll suffice. See, that wasn't so bad. And thank you for your business sir!

OVER THE TOP TIM: What do you mean I didn't thank you?

ME: Well, you said thanks for the directions, not thank you for your service, but I'll let it go.

OVER THE TOP TIM: Sounds like you are knit picking a bit now, aren't you?

ME: Not really, you just gave me a lesser thank you than we all agreed upon.

OVER THE TOP TIM: I didn't agree to anything!

RESERVIST #2: You kinda did.

Over the Top Tim stormed away confused and frazzled while the reservists and I laughed mightily.

RESERVIST #2: I can't wait to get back to the base to tell this story!

ME: I thought it was pretty funny myself! But seriously guys, how do you feel about the "Thank you for your service" from random people?

RESERVIST #1: It's a nice gesture, but sometimes disingenuous and over the top like with that guy, I think he was looking for attention.

RESERVIST #2: I'm not a huge fan of it, I mean that's what I decided to do, maybe thank me on Veteran's Day or something. There are plenty of jobs that deserve lots of thanks, like my kid's teacher. Shit, I wouldn't want that job, I can't handle him, let alone 20 others all day!

RESERVIST #1: Good to see you, we'll see you next week and oh, (*extending his hand for a handshake*) thank you for your service!

ME: *Now really laughing.* You guys usually enjoy my parking lot stories, now you're in one!

RESERVIST #2: That guy still doesn't know what hit him!

The three reservists walked away laughing. As they got to the corner and were waiting for the light to change so they could cross the street over to the restaurants, I opened my door and yelled hey guys, THANK YOU FOR YOUR SERVICE! The people that were on the corner with them waiting for the light, now feeling obligated, turned to them and started thanking them for their service as well. A loud laugh erupted as the light turned and they went on to enjoy their Friday lunch.

While we all got a good laugh together from the encounter with Over the Top Tim, we should all be thankful for what the members of the military do and the sacrifices they make. We should also be thankful for all of the other professions that make a difference for us each and every day. Teachers, nurses, doctors, firefighters, and police, to name just a few. Feel free to show your thanks, just do not be an attention seeking tool about it, like Over the Top Tim.

Concealed Confusion

During my time at the parking lot, I dealt with somewhere around 120,000 people. Some were repeat customers, but it was 120,000 cars nonetheless. People came to the parking lot for different reasons, many of which involved a trip to court that was not by choice, such as traffic tickets, code violations, small claims lawsuits, child custody issues, divorces, and criminal cases. Some people came to court on their own free will because they needed a copy of a marriage license, information about filing a case, and, the most frequent reason, to renew or obtain a concealed carry firearm license.

In the South, concealed carry licenses are as common as driver's licenses. Everyone's packing heat down here. I had to keep that in mind when I first moved here from New York and was still car horn happy out on the roads. In New York, honking a horn at someone for the smallest thing was commonplace. Up North, you would blow the horn at someone, exchange a few pleasantries, and go on your way. Not so much here in the South with everyone packing, so I had to adjust my driving habits accordingly. You do not want to piss off someone who is carrying a firearm in their console, glove box, or on their waistband. So, you make adjustments. Shit, I am a New Yorker and I even got a concealed carry permit, it is just something you do down here.

Obtaining a concealed carry permit is quite simple here. You go down to the courthouse, fill out an application, get your picture taken, pay a fee, get your fingerprints taken and then wait a couple of weeks for a background check. Simple and easy. If all goes well, you will have a carry permit in a few weeks. There are no written tests about gun laws, and no tests that involve your skills with a gun, your mental capacity, or things of that nature. If you do not have a felony background or a mental hospital commitment in your past, you can get a permit. Even if you do not have a concealed carry permit in Georgia, you can still carry a weapon on your person, in plain sight; you just cannot conceal it under your clothes or in a purse. You can also carry a firearm in your vehicle without a permit, as your car is considered an extension of your home for purposes of gun laws. A concealed carry license is just that, a license to keep your weapon concealed. So, at the parking lot, I had a couple dozen customers daily coming to go to court to renew or obtain a concealed carry permit, even an occasional senior "cowboy."

CONFUSED COWBOY CLINT: *Waving a gun, wearing a cowboy hat.* Is this where I get one of them carry permits for this here gun?

ME: Sir, not a good idea to be walking around with that gun like that!

CONFUSED COWBOY CLINT: Oh, that's why I am here, to get a permit to carry it around!

ME: Ok, well sir, you'll need to leave it in your car.

CONFUSED COWBOY CLINT: Oh, I can't bring it on inside?

ME: No sir, if you walk through those doors waving a gun, you'll probably get shot.

CONFUSED COWBOY CLINT: You wanna hold it up in there for me?

ME: No sir, I cannot hold your gun for you, you have to leave it in the car.

CONFUSED COWBOY CLINT: Should I unload it?

ME: I think you should gently place it in your glove box.

CONFUSED COWBOY CLINT: Ok, I'll get right back with ya.

Confused Cowboy Clint, having trouble walking because of his ripe old age, moseyed on back to his truck that was parked crooked in two spaces and placed the loaded pistol in his glove box. He then returned a few minutes later.

CONFUSED COWBOY CLINT: You know anything about these here gun permits?

ME: What would you like to know sir?

CONFUSED COWBOY CLINT: *Reaching in his overalls pocket.* Well, I got me here the application copied out from the computer. I need to fill the darn thing out! You got a pen up in there? I wanna get this done so I'm all legal. Don't wanna be bellying through the brush if ya know what I mean!

ME: Yes, sir, here you go,

Confused Cowboy Clint, pen in his left hand, reached for his eyeglasses with his very shaky right hand and put them on. His lenses were so thick; I was certain he could see the rings of Saturn on a clear night.

CONFUSED COWBOY CLINT: Can I fill it out here on your shelf so you can help me if I need it?

ME: Sure sir.

CONFUSED COWBOY CLINT: Ok, first name, last name, got that. Ok, date. It's what, June...

ME: July.

CONFUSED COWBOY CLINT: Juuuly? No more June?

ME: No sir, it is July eleventh.

CONFUSED COWBOY CLINT: Wow, where did June go? Ok, Juuuly the eleventh, 2009.

ME: No sir, it is 2017!

CONFUSED COWBOY CLINT: 2017?! What am I thinking? You sure?

ME: I am certain it is 2017, sir.

CONFUSED COWBOY CLINT: Ok, address, got that, date of birth and all that, I think I got it all.

ME: *Looking at his application, with penmanship that was almost illegible from his shaking hand.* I think you got everything.

CONFUSED COWBOY CLINT: Now, how much do I owe you for the parking?

ME: It is five dollars, sir.

CONFUSED COWBOY CLINT: *Searching his overalls for his wallet.* Got it! Ok, here's a five, am I good to go?

ME: No sir, this is a fifty-dollar bill, you made a mistake, do you want me to break this or do you have a smaller bill?

CONFUSED COWBOY CLINT: Oh darn it, that looked like a five-dollar bill, I think I got one in here! Is this a five?

ME: No sir, that's a twenty-dollar bill!

CONFUSED COWBOY CLINT: Oh, my eyes ain't what they used to be! Oh, here's a five!

ME: That's ok sir, yup that's a five! You are all set!

CONFUSED COWBOY CLINT: Now where do I go?

ME: The building directly across the street, the big brown one.

CONFUSED COWBOY CLINT: That one?

ME: Yes, sir, that's the one!

CONFUSED COWBOY CLINT: Thanks for your help young man! Can't wait to get the permit! Don't wanna be a blatherskite and talk your ears off!

ME: You're the most excited I've ever seen someone about getting a concealed carry permit.

CONFUSED COWBOY CLINT: Because then I can stop one of them big mass shootings at a restaurant or wherever I am at. He'll be sorry he messed with me!

ME: Well, hopefully you'll never have to deal with that sir!

CONFUSED COWBOY CLINT: Me neither, but I will be prepared! I will draw my weapon and that'll be the end of him! I'll be a hero on the news! You might see me someday! Nobody gonna bushwhack me!

Confused Cowboy Clint walked away, around the corner and into the wrong building. A few minutes later I saw him cross into the correct building. I sat there feeling a bit bad for him. He was clearly confused, had poor eyesight, did not know what date (or year) it was, could not give me the proper bill denomination, parked crooked, and was completely out of sorts. We are all going to get old, so I had compassion and helped him out the best I could. What I could not understand is how this guy was going to be allowed to carry a concealed gun, or any gun for that matter. He had no reflexes, minimal eyesight, very unsteady hands, and very little judgment as he initially approached me waving a gun. I was hoping someone in there would talk him out of carrying a gun because, like the great cowboy Kenny Rogers once said, "You gotta know when to hold 'em, know when to fold 'em, know when to walk away." This cowboy's time of rootin', tootin', and shootin' were clearly behind him. No such luck for the general population as Confused Cowboy Clint came out thirty or so minutes later happy as a pig in shit.

CONFUSED COWBOY CLINT: I'll have it in a few weeks!

ME: That's great sir, congratulations.

CONFUSED COWBOY CLINT: This town is gonna be safer now!

ME: So I can rest easy now, huh?

CONFUSED COWBOY CLINT: Damn straight, time to take the country back!

ME: Maybe just start with the town, you know, baby steps.

CONFUSED COWBOY CLINT: Y'all hiring here? Maybe I can do security for you.

ME: No, we're good sir, but thanks for thinking of us.

CONFUSED COWBOY CLINT: *Rummaging through his pockets.* Did I leave my keys with you?

ME: No, sir.

CONFUSED COWBOY CLINT: I ain't got 'em! Where could I have left them?

ME: Did you lock them in your car when you put your gun away? Or maybe you left them in the bin when you went through the metal detector inside the courthouse?

CONFUSED COWBOY CLINT: Must've left 'em inside 'cause I ain't got my wallet neither! Guess I gotta go back inside!

ME: Well, good luck sir! Hope you find them!

Confused Cowboy Clint came out of the courthouse for a second time, this time waving his keys and wallet to show me he found them.

CONFUSED COWBOY CLINT: I found 'em!

ME: Great sir, you take care now!

CONFUSED COWBOY CLINT: How do I get out of here?

ME: Same way you came in, down the hill. There are two big exits by that big sign.

CONFUSED COWBOY CLINT: Where? I can't see that far anymore!

ME: See that big sign down there? The one that says parking with the big red arrow?

CONFUSED COWBOY CLINT: Can't see that far, I'll see it when I drive down there.

ME: Ummmmm, ok, be careful.

CONFUSED COWBOY CLINT: See ya buddy!

Confused Cowboy Clint slowly circled the lot a couple of times like he was rounding up cattle, until he was finally able to locate one of the four exits. Happy trails Cowboy Clint, until we meet again.

Food Frenzy

Food seemed to be on the minds of the vast majority of parking lot customers. People constantly asked where they could get coffee, breakfast, lunch, snacks, and anything else they could get their hands on. The fact that most people were always "running late" and didn't have time to stop for something on their way in, combined with the fact that there are a dozen or so restaurants in the immediate area of the parking lot that emitted various aromas from morning until night, fueled their food frenzy. Of course, I had to field dozens of questions per day about these various food smells.

ME: Good afternoon ma'am! Can I help you?

FINGER LICKIN' LINDA: I just got out of court and I am starving! What's that smell of food in the air?

ME: Probably the deli on the corner or one of the restaurants down the street.

FINGER LICKIN' LINDA: Is that fried chicken I smell?

ME: Ma'am, I have no idea.

FINGER LICKIN' LINDA: *Eyes open wider than Ralph Kramden's.* Do you think it is fried chicken? Where can I get fried chicken?

ME: I truly have no idea, ma'am.

FINGER LICKIN' LINDA: Well, don't you work here? You must know all the places and what they serve, no?

ME: Ma'am, I know the names of most of the restaurants but I haven't been to many. I've been here almost two years and I've never gotten a lunch break.

FINGER LICKIN' LINDA: *Not interested in my working conditions.* But, any idea about the fried chicken?

ME: No idea.

FINGER LICKIN' LINDA: I'm really in the mood for fried chicken now, it's gotta be close by! Can you look it up? It is making me crazy!

ME: Let me look at my fried chicken GPS app.

FINGER LICKIN' LINDA: *Missing my sarcasm.* Ok, great!

ME: Ma'am I was joking, there is no app for locating fried chicken.

FINGER LICKIN' LINDA: Can you Google fried chicken and the name of the town we're in? It'll come up!

ME: I am sorry ma'am, I just can't. I have other people behind you to help with their parking.

FINGER LICKIN' LINDA: Oh shucks, guess I am gonna have to walk around until I find where that smell is coming from! I won't quit until I find it!

Finger Lickin' Linda went off on her fried chicken expedition. She returned about an hour later, carrying an open sheet of aluminum foil with a couple of pieces of fried chicken on it.

FINGER LICKIN' LINDA: *Gnawing on a fried chicken thigh.* Found it! In case anyone asks, it is that little place around the block that serves breakfast and lunch. It is soooo good! Wanna try?

ME: Ummmm, no thanks, I am good.

FINGER LICKIN' LINDA: You're missing out! Come on, try.

ME: *Thinking of an excuse.* Sorry ma'am, I'm vegan!

FINGER LICKIN' LINDA: You vegans are all crazy! Nothing wrong with meat! We been eating meat since the cavemen, now people have a problem with meat!

ME: Well enjoy your day ma'am, glad you found the chicken place!

FINGER LICKIN' LINDA: *In mid chew, spitting chicken while speaking.* Thanks! Me too!

The cuisine questioning was not limited to fried chicken, and it transcended that of mere fried finger foods.

FUNNEL CAKE FRANKIE: I'm parked in spot 55, how much is it?

ME: It is five dollars to park, sir.

FUNNEL CAKE FRANKIE: Wow, I smell funnel cakes!

ME: Funnel cakes?

FUNNEL CAKE FRANKIE: Yeah! Any idea where that smell is coming from?

ME: No idea, probably one of the restaurants, doubtful it is funnel cake though. I'm not aware of anyone that serves them around here.

FUNNEL CAKE FRANKIE: Oh it's funnel cake!

ME: Ummmm...ok.

FUNNEL CAKE FRANKIE: Is there a festival going on in town today? A circus maybe?

ME: Well sir, festivals only happen here in town on the weekends, so it is definitely not a festival. As far as the circus, the only circus in town is in this parking lot and I'm definitely not serving any funnel cakes.

FUNNEL CAKE FRANKIE: I'm telling you it is funnel cake!

ME: I'll take your word for it.

Funnel Cake Frankie paid for his parking and then felt it was necessary to ask each person that he crossed paths with whether or not they smelled the funnel cake and whether or not they knew where he could get said funnel cake. Frankie came up short on his funnel cake crusade. An hour or so later he left court still in his self-inflicted fried dough dilemma.

It was not always about the search for food, sometimes it was about the food that people brought with them, especially in the early mornings.

ME: Good Morning sir, how are you today?

BREAKFAST BURRITO BILLY: *Chomping on an oversized gas station breakfast burrito.* Good Morning, how much for the parking?

ME: It is five dollars, sir.

BREAKFAST BURRITO BILLY: Can you hold this?

ME: Hold what?

BREAKFAST BURRITO BILLY: My burrito, I have to reach and get my wallet and money.

ME: Ummmm...no sir.

BREAKFAST BURRITO BILLY: Why the hell not?!

ME: Well, you don't even have any foil or wax paper around the burrito, I'd be holding your actual tortilla.

BREAKFAST BURRITO BILLY: So what?

ME: So, it's kind of disgusting.

BREAKFAST BURRITO BILLY: What's disgusting about it?

ME: First off, you just had it in your mouth, now you want me to handle it. Secondly, how is it that you want my hands to make direct contact with something you're about to eat?

BREAKFAST BURRITO BILLY: Doesn't bother me none!

ME: How do you know I didn't just use the restroom and failed to wash my hands?

BREAKFAST BURRITO BILLY: Well, you are gonna touch my credit card, then I'm gonna touch it and then touch my burrito again so it don't make much difference now does it?

ME: Well, you're much more liberal with your food handling policies than I am.

BREAKFAST BURRITO BILLY: What do you mean liberal? I ain't no liberal!

ME: Sir, I didn't mean politically. Liberal in this sense, means you are loose, or not strict about your food handling rules.

BREAKFAST BURRITO BILLY: Oh, I was never called a liberal before! So, you can't hold it?

ME: No.

Billy decided that stuffing the remaining third of his breakfast burrito in his mouth to free up his hands was a better option than just finishing his burrito and then paying for his parking. As cheese, egg and other unidentified burrito ingredients fell from his mouth when he attempted to chew a piece of burrito the size of a baseball card, Billy reached for his wallet and handed me his debit card. I processed his transaction faster than he could chew and swallow that remaining slab of breakfast goodness. At least Billy's mouth was too full to ask a stupid follow up question about funnel cakes and fried chicken.

In the springtime, there are nonstop ads on television for the Georgia Renaissance Festival, which takes place in a town not far from the parking lot. I've never met a person in my life that has gone to a Renaissance Festival. However, I do know that people dress in stupid looking costumes, act out dumb shit, and eat weird foods at these festivals. Not my kind of thing, but to each their own. One Monday morning, a woman approached the booth who had clearly been at the Renaissance Festival that past weekend:

ME: Good morning ma'am, how are you today?

RENAISSANCE RITA: *Wearing a Renaissance Fair t-shirt.* Ok I guess! Sucks it is Monday!

ME: I know! Paying for parking? What space are you in?

RENAISSANCE RITA: *Biting into a humungous turkey leg the size of my arm.* Space 66!

ME: Ummmm, ok. Are you paying by cash or card?

RENAISSANCE RITA: Card, hey let me ask you something. Are they gonna let me in court with this?

ME: With what, ma'am?

RENAISSANCE RITA: My turkey leg! I don't want it going to waste, I still got a lot of meat left up on the bone!

ME: I am honestly not sure, but I do know that anything going into court has to go through the x-ray scanner.

RENAISSANCE RITA: They're gonna x-ray my turkey leg?

ME: Most likely.

RENAISSANCE RITA: For what? What the fuck can I hide in a turkey leg?

ME: No idea ma'am, razor blades perhaps. It is just court policy that anything going inside has to be scanned. No need to curse at me.

RENAISSANCE RITA: I apologize, but why would you suggest that I would put razor blades in my turkey leg and ruin good meat? That's the dumbest thing I ever heard!

ME: I'm just speculating on razor blades, ma'am, and what they'd be looking for. And besides, that thing is so big, it could be used as a weapon. It's the size of a baseball bat! Maybe you should finish your turkey leg before you go in.

RENAISSANCE RITA: That's the whole idea of these turkey legs, they're big! That's the selling point! Do you know how long it is gonna take to pick this big bone clean and get all this meat off?

ME: I have no idea ma'am; I've never timed someone eating a giant turkey leg.

RENAISSANCE RITA: At least half an hour!

ME: Let me ask you, why would you bring a giant turkey leg to court?

RENAISSANCE RITA: It's my goddamn breakfast, did you have YOUR breakfast today!?

ME: Actually, no.

RENAISSANCE RITA: Well that's too bad, but this is my breakfast and I don't want it going to waste! I saved it specifically for breakfast today!

ME: Well, then it appears that you have a few choices. Finish it, take your chances bringing it inside, or leave it in the car.

RENAISSANCE RITA: None are great options! I want to eat it inside court while I'm waiting for my case to be heard.

ME: Well, I have no control over any of that, I work in the parking lot. I have no control over what happens inside or about courthouse turkey leg rules and regulations.

RENAISSANCE RITA: Well, you're no help. Let me pay for my spot and I'll figure it all out.

Renaissance Rita paid for her parking then decided to lean against her car gnawing on that Fred Flintstone-sized turkey leg for about twenty minutes until the bone was all but picked clean. Of course, I found the carcass the next morning in the lot when I did my morning clean up. Like there was ever a doubt.

The food frenzy continued a few weeks later when a woman wearing a blouse and skirt three sizes too small approached the window with her version of a balanced breakfast.

ME: Good morning ma'am, nice day today, huh?

BREAKFAST COMBO CAROL: *Slurping on an oversized hot chocolate with a mound of whipped cream on top.* Sure is!

ME: Will you be paying credit or cash today?

BREAKFAST COMBO CAROL: *Taking an enormous bite out of a slice of gas station supreme pizza.* Credit, parking space number 68!

Breakfast Combo Carol placed her gargantuan hot chocolate and supreme slice of pizza down on the outside shelf and fumbled for her credit card.

BREAKFAST COMBO CAROL: Here you go!

ME: You are all set, here's your receipt. Have a great day!

BREAKFAST COMBO CAROL: *Chewing pizza.* How do I get to the nomnomnomnom court?

ME: I'm sorry ma'am, where do you need to go?

BREAKFAST COMBO CAROL: *Taking another colossal bite of pizza.* To nomnomnomnomnom court!

ME: I can't understand you, ma'am.

BREAKFAST COMBO CAROL: You got a hearing problem? Or you just don't know where shit is?

ME: No, I just can't understand you with half a slice of fully loaded supreme pizza in your mouth. It's rude to talk with a mouth full of food!

BREAKFAST COMBO CAROL: *Unfazed and not willing to miss a bite of pizza.* You are nomnomnomnom fucking rude!

ME: I'm rude? You're devouring an oversized gas station slice of pizza and sucking down a gallon of cocoa at 8:00 am while asking questions, and I'm the rude one?

BREAKFAST COMBO CAROL: Fuck off, you aren't my boss! Rude ass bitch!

Breakfast Combo Carol stormed off, still enjoying her breakfast of champions. As she got to the corner across from the courthouse, I noticed that she threw the triangular shaped cardboard pizza slice box on the ground. She continued walking to court while slurping down her big gulp sized hot chocolate with the avalanche of whipped cream on top. When the morning rush died down, I went over and picked up her cardboard pizza box. I walked over to space number 68 where she was parked and jammed the pizza box into her wheel well.

A few hours passed and Breakfast Combo Carol strolled towards her car, this time with a large soda and a hot dog from the nearby deli. She was now transformed into Lunch Combo Carol. Carol walked down to her car while inhaling her hot dog and chugging, what I am certain, was a diet soda. She started up her car and started to drive away but then suddenly stopped. She got out of her car and looked around at each tire. The pizza box I jammed into the wheel well earlier must have been making a rubbing sound, which caused her to think that perhaps she had a flat tire. She got back into the car, drove a few more feet, then stopped again. She got out and did another walking, visual inspection of her vehicle, but found nothing. Lunch Combo Carol then picked up her cell phone and called someone. I could clearly hear her explain to the person that her car was making a funny noise, like a friction sound. She then told the person that she could be there in fifteen minutes and asked if she could be taken at that time. It seemed as though Lunch Combo Carol placed a call to a local mechanic. Later that afternoon, I could not help but wonder if the pizza symbol light on Lunch Combo Carol's dash had lit up telling her it was just her pizza box, or if the mechanic's diagnostic machine picked up a pizza box trouble code. Either way, Lunch Combo Carol brought it on herself by being rude and littering. It was just another case of parking lot justice served, this time, with the works.

The Candy Conniver

As noted above, around the holidays each year, at my own expense, I put out a large bowl of candy for the customers to enjoy -- usually individually wrapped soft peppermint puff candies. I thought it was a nice gesture and hoped that it would put people in some sort of holiday spirit. Within an hour of putting out the first big bowl of them, people started grabbing handfuls of candy, so much so that it forced me to tape a sign to the bowl that read "Please Take ONE." I knew this would not stop everyone from being a glutton, but hoped it would help. A week before Christmas a middle aged man came up to the window.

CHILDLESS CHUCK: Good morning, ooooh candy!

ME: Good morning sir, yes take one and enjoy!

CHILDLESS CHUCK: *Putting one in his mouth*. These are good!

ME: Glad you like them! Will you be paying cash or card for your parking today?

CHILDLESS CHUCK: Cash, here you go. Spot 33.

ME: Thank you, sir, here's your ticket. Have a happy holiday!

CHILDLESS CHUCK: You too! I'm gonna take some more of these for my three kids (*grabbing two handfuls of candies*)!

ME: *Staring in disgust*.

CHILDLESS CHUCK: What's wrong? Am I supposed to go back to the car eating candy and not give my kids any?

ME: I didn't say anything, sir.

CHILDLESS CHUCK: But you looked at me all pissed off.

ME: That's my default resting face sir. Where are your kids?

CHILDLESS CHUCK: Ummmmm, in the car.

ME: Ok, hope they enjoy the candy.

Childless Chuck started to walk away, only to be stopped by a woman he knew. They proceeded to have a conversation right in front of my booth.

HONEST HOLLY: Chuck! How have you been?

CHILDLESS CHUCK: Hey Holly, I'm good!

HONEST HOLLY: Things going ok? I'm sorry about how things ended there.

CHILDLESS CHUCK: Onto bigger and better things, I start after the holidays!

HONEST HOLLY: Well I hope everything works out over there for you. How's your Mom?

CHILDLESS CHUCK: She's good! How's your family?

HONEST HOLLY: Everyone is great, getting set for the holidays!

CHILDLESS CHUCK: Well, I gotta get inside, nice seeing you!

HONEST HOLLY: Nice seeing you too Chuck, say hi to your mom!

Chuck ran off to court and right past his parking space number 33, which was three spots away from my booth. No kids were in the car, nor did he stop to get his kids. Could he have lied about having kids in order to bilk candy from me?

ME: Good morning, ma'am.

HONEST HOLLY: Good morning, the decorations you put up are so nice! All set for Christmas?

ME: Yes, how about you?

HONEST HOLLY: Getting there! You take cards, right?

ME: Sure do! Can I ask you something?

HONEST HOLLY: Yeah, sure.

ME: That guy you were just chatting with…

HONEST HOLLY: Chuck?

ME: Yeah, do you know him well?

HONEST HOLLY: Pretty well. He worked with me for three years, he was just let go a couple of weeks ago. Felt bad for him, getting laid off right around the holidays, but he found another job already. It worked out for him. I know his Mom too. Why do you ask?

ME: Does he have three kids?

HONEST HOLLY: No. He does not have any kids. He lives with his Mom. He's not married or anything either.

ME: I knew it!

HONEST HOLLY: Knew it?

ME: Long story, but he just raided the candy dish and said he had three kids in the car. I had a feeling he was lying; I did not see any kids.

HONEST HOLLY: Sounds like something Chuck would do, he used to take supplies from the office. That's why they let him go.

ME: Interesting. Well, here's your receipt. Thanks so much for the info, and have a happy holiday!

HONEST HOLLY: You too, thanks! Sorry Chuck stole all your candy!

ME: No worries!

Ok, so Chuck had sticky fingers, and not from the individually wrapped mints. Not the crime of the century, but who lies about having kids to justify candy thievery? "Let it go Charlie, it is Christmastime" said the angel on my left shoulder. "Call that motherfucker out" said the devil on my right shoulder. Or was it the opposite? I don't recall. Anyway, I couldn't stop myself from bringing it up when Childless Chuck came out of court.

ME: *Yelling out the booth door.* Chuck!

CHILDLESS CHUCK: *Startled.* Me?

ME: Yeah, come on by for a second.

CHILDLESS CHUCK: Do I owe you more money?

ME: No. Where are your kids?

CHILDLESS CHUCK: Inside with my wife, I have to pick them up by the exit.

ME: Did they enjoy the mints?

CHILDLESS CHUCK: *Turning towards his car.* Ummm, yeah, thanks again! Merry Christmas!

ME: You know, I had a little conversation with Holly while you were in court.

CHILDLESS CHUCK: Who is Holly? I don't know any Holly.

ME: The lady you used to work with, the one you chatted with before.

CHILDLESS CHUCK: Oh, that Holly, of course, yeah nice lady.

ME: Holly said you don't have any wife or kids.

CHILDLESS CHUCK: Why are you so concerned about me and my kids, and now my wife?

ME: Well, come on Chuck, you took the candy for yourself. Come on, just admit it.

CHILDLESS CHUCK: Are you the fucking candy police?

ME: No, but I did do a little digging, and Holly told me all about the office supplies, the kids, or lack thereof, and some other stuff.

CHILDLESS CHUCK: You're insane, all because of a handful of mints?

ME: It's not really about the mints Chuck, it's about the conniving.

CHILDLESS CHUCK: So what are you going to do, arrest me for taking extra fucking mints?

ME: No arrest Chuck, just wanted you to know that I knew all along that those mints were all for you!

CHILDLESS CHUCK: Don't you have anything better to do all day?

ME: This is what I do Chuck, I enforce unwritten social rules.

CHILDLESS CHUCK: No, you police candy dishes!

ME: Ok Chuck, good luck at the new job! Don't be taking shit from the stockroom!

CHILDLESS CHUCK: Fuck off you piece of shit! You're lucky you're in there or I'd kick your ass!

ME: Wish the wife and kids a Merry Christmas for me!

Chuck sprung into his car, and let out a whistle, and away he flew, like a heat seeking missile, but I heard him exclaim as he drove out of sight "Fuck all y'all, and get a fucking life."

Condensed Courthouse Chronicles

There were many shorter, less complicated, interactions during my time at the lot. Although they are not long stories, I feel they are definitely good for a few laughs. The following are some of my favorites.

Bobbitt Buffoonery

One morning, a 40-something year old man approached the payment booth. He thought he had the joke of the century and had a captive audience of me and seven or so people on line to test out his joke.

OLD JOKE JAKE: I'm running so late! There was a crash on I-75!

ME: That's terrible, hope everyone was ok.

OLD JOKE JAKE: Unfortunately, not! Remember that woman Lorena Bobbit?

ME: Yeah, the one who cut off her husband's privates!

OLD JOKE JAKE: Yeah, that's the one. She died in the accident!

ME: Did some dick cut her off?

Everyone laughed, except for Old Joke Jake.

OLD JOKE JAKE: How did you know that the punchline? I made that one up!

ME: Sir, with all due respect, I heard that joke back when I was still dancing to "Whoomp! There It Is" and wearing Drakkar cologne.

Everyone laughed heartily again, except Old Joke Jake who walked away dejected. He had the joke of the century alright, the 20th century.

Inside Looking In

One late morning, a man carrying a wire hanger approached the payment window.

WIRE HANGER WILLIE: Hey man, I am parked here, paid this morning over in spot 82.

ME: Ok sir, is everything ok?

WIRE HANGER WILLIE: Well just wanted you to know that my keys are locked in and I'm trying to get them out with this wire hanger. Didn't want you to think I was breaking into cars.

ME: Well, thanks for letting me know sir, I appreciate it.

WIRE HANGER WILLIE: Thank God I had this wire hanger in the back of my minivan so I have something to try and get in the car with!

ME: Wait, if your car was locked with the keys inside, how did you get in the back of the minivan for the wire hanger?

WIRE HANGER WILLIE: Oh my God! I am an idiot! I could have just climbed to the front and gotten the keys while I got the hanger, now even the back is locked! Guess I'll try the hanger!

Dewey Decimal Dumbass

Every Monday morning, the town was overrun with new pools of jurors summoned for jury duty. The county had very limited parking for jurors, and when the jury parking lot was full, the jurors would scramble all over looking for parking. Their summonses clearly stated that if the jury lot was full, the jury overflow lot was at the public library, which was an enormous building just two blocks away. Very few read their summonses. Each Monday chaos ensued. Even those that did read the summonses were still not all that bright.

ME: Good morning ma'am, can I help you?

JACKASS JUROR JULIE: I'm a juror.

ME: Ok.

JACKASS JUROR JULIE: The guy at the jury lot told me to park here since they were full.

ME: I am not sure why he directed you here ma'am, we are a privately owned lot, you'll have to pay five dollars to park here. The free overflow juror parking is at the public library. It's all spelled out on your jury summons.

JACKASS JUROR JULIE: These summonses are so confusing. I know they have a map on them and all, but they should have a big star on them that says "YOU ARE HERE" so you can get your bearings and know how to get to the parking lots and court from your starting point.

ME: Ma'am, how would the summons know where you are? It's a preprinted summons for everyone, not everyone is starting from the same point. But anyway, the overflow lot is at the library.

JACKASS JUROR JULIE: I know, that's why I am here.

ME: I'm not quite sure I understand.

JACKASS JUROR JULIE: *Pointing to the 8' x 8' tiny shack I am* in. This is the public library, right?

ME: *Laughing.* No, ma'am, this is a tiny payment building for this parking lot.

JACKASS JUROR JULIE: What's so funny?! Anyone could mistake this for the library!

ME: Ma'am, the building I am in is the size of a tool shed, what could you possibly fit inside here, five books and a laptop?

JACKASS JUROR JULIE: Ok, maybe an auxiliary library then!

ME: So, three books then? Anyway, the library is up the block at the second traffic light on the right.

JACKASS JUROR JULIE: Fine, maybe they'll be nicer over there!

Ok, so maybe I made Jackass Juror Julie feel a bit silly, but in all seriousness, this woman was selected to make a life changing decision on a jury as to whether someone is going to go to jail, possibly to the electric chair, and she thought a tiny shack in a parking lot was the public library. Shit, I hope my life never rests in the hands of a jury.

Quick Lube Lot

A few times a week, I arrived at work to find cars that were illegally parked in the parking lot overnight that had no ticket in the window. I would usually give the person who left the vehicle a full work day to come and get it before having it towed and impounded. A courtesy I did not have to give, but extended to most people anyway. Sometimes I wish I had not.

ME: Good afternoon sir, how's it going today?

OIL CHANGE CHARLIE: Good, I am here to work on a car.

ME: Work on a car?

OIL CHANGE CHARLIE: Uh yeah, my friend left his car here overnight, it wouldn't start when he left court late yesterday.

ME: Oh ok, I know the car. You looking to get it started and off the lot?

OIL CHANGE CHARLIE: Yeah, I am going to do that, an oil change, maybe tune it up for him, top off the fluids...

ME: Wait, what? Oil change and tune up?

OIL CHANGE CHARLIE: Yeah, is that a problem?

ME: Yes, sir, I can't have oil changes and tune ups done here. Just get it started and off the lot.

OIL CHANGE CHARLIE: I don't see what the big deal is!

ME: Sir, I am running a business here. I already lost money on that spot because I could not sell it this morning. Now you want it to sit here while you perform incidental work on the car. I can't have it. I need it started and off the lot.

OIL CHANGE CHARLIE: You guys are too fucking strict here!

ME: Name a business that would allow you to do an oil change on their premises. It's not really up for debate, no oil changes or tune ups, just get it started or I'll have to call the tow truck.

OIL CHANGE CHARLIE: Fine!

Oil Change Charlie struggled for about an hour to get the vehicle started with no success. When he finally gave up and left, I called the tow truck and had his pal's car towed to the impound yard like I should have done when I arrived that morning. Perhaps the impound yard allowed him to do that much needed oil change and tune up on their premises and included a couple of quarts of oil with their 175-dollar tow and impound fee.

Power Payment

I'll admit, the signage in our parking lot left a lot, pun intended, to be desired. Some of it was confusing, some had extraneous information, and some did not have enough information. But the one thing the owners were sure to make clear to everyone, or at least try to, was where to pay. There were signs that said "PAY AT BOOTH" all over the parking lot. "PAY AT BOOTH" signs were at all of the entrances and along the perimeter of the lot. A printed awning at the booth (shack, hut, whatever the fuck it was) said "PAY HERE" in the biggest lettering I ever saw. So, you would think it would be crystal clear to everyone just where to pay for their parking spot. You would think. During my tenure at the parking lot, I witnessed people attempting to pay county road workers, police, other customers, truck drivers making local deliveries, and even landscapers. The most entertaining payment attempt came one spring morning when an older gentleman exited his vehicle, looked around, and headed straight for the side street where a Georgia Power utility worker was in up his cherry picker, forty feet off the ground, working on the power lines.

POWER PAYER PAUL: *Looking up at the cherry picker and waving a five-dollar bill*: HEEEEEEEEY! You up there!

GEORGIA POWER GUY: Me?

POWER PAYER PAUL: I got your money!

GEORGIA POWER GUY: What? I can barely hear you!

POWER PAYER PAUL: I got your five dollars!

GEORGIA POWER GUY: I don't know what you are talking about!

POWER PAYER PAUL: For the parking! Should I leave it on your windshield?!

GEORGIA POWER GUY: Parking?! I work for Georgia Power! I'm working the lines!

POWER PAYER PAUL: I know you're busy, so just leave it on your windshield?!

GEORGIA POWER GUY: I don't take money for parking! I work for the power company!

POWER PAYER PAUL: I know, isn't it all related, utilities, courts, all state or county stuff?

GEORGIA POWER GUY: No! I work for the power company! I don't handle parking!

POWER PAYER PAUL: Oh! Where do I pay then?

GEORGIA POWER GUY: *Pointing in my direction.* Probably at that building that says "Pay Here" on it!

Power Payer Paul, with the help of the linesman, figured out where to pay and then went on his way. When the Georgia Power worker finished and lowered himself to the ground I went over to him and told him that I dealt with stupidity like that all day, every day. He was greatly amused by the whole thing and said it would make a great story for his fellow workers. And a great story for a book, Georgia Power Guy.

Tax Time Toyota

Early spring brings thoughts of vacations, warm weather, titty money, and tax time. Taxes were on the minds of a few customers in my final spring at the lot. As a matter of fact, a SUV with dark, tinted windows pulled into the parking lot one March morning with two decals affixed to it that read "Tax Refund

Processed Here" and "File Your Taxes Here, Then Drive Home."
Seems legit -- no company name, no phone number, a rusted out
SUV, dark tint on the windows -- who could ask for more?
Certainly nobody would take this guy up on his offer, or would
they?

ME: Good Morning, Sir!

AUTOMOBILE TAX ADVISOR: I'm paying for two spaces, numbers
26 and 27.

ME: Sure sir, that'll be ten dollars.

AUTOMOBILE TAX ADVISOR: Can I get a receipt; I need it for my
business.

ME: Coming right up, sir.

AUTOMOBILE TAX ADVISOR: Just to let you know, I'm not going
to court or anything, I'll be in my vehicle preparing a client's taxes
with him, he's the other spot I paid for.

ME: No problem sir, they are your spots, you can do anything you
like in them, within the law, of course.

AUTOMOBILE TAX ADVISOR: Of course! Shouldn't be more than
an hour.

ME: No worries, have a good day!

About thirty minutes later, the Automobile Tax Advisor came
back up to the payment window, laptop in hand, with his client
standing behind him.

AUTOMOBILE TAX ADVISOR: Do you think we could come inside
so I can finish his taxes?

ME: Come inside where?

AUTOMOBILE TAX ADVISOR: Where you are, in that booth.

ME: I'm sorry sir, but for security reasons, I cannot allow anyone in here.

AUTOMOBILE TAX ADVISOR: It'll only be a few minutes, my laptop battery is dead, I just need to plug in and finish. Plus, it is hot as hell in the car! You sell iced coffee? Oh, and do you have a printer I can connect to in there to print out the documents?

ME: No sir, I do not sell beverages of any kind, and again, I cannot allow you inside here. And no, I do not have a printer.

AUTOMOBILE TAX ADVISOR: Tell you what, you let me in, I'll do your taxes for half price!

ME: So tempting sir, but I had my taxes done about a month ago.

AUTOMOBILE TAX ADVISOR: Come on, don't be a hard ass!

ME: Sir, with all due respect, isn't it embarrassing enough that you are preparing taxes in a parking lot inside a beat up SUV? Now you want to do them in a shack in a parking lot? Why don't you take your client to a coffee shop so you can have your iced coffee, all the power for your laptop that you need and a nice atmosphere?

AUTOMOBILE TAX ADVISOR: Alright, I don't want to argue in front of my customer. We'll go to Starbuck's! Thanks for nothing! Can I have my ten dollars back?

ME: Ten dollars back? For your parking?

AUTOMOBILE TAX ADVISOR: Yes, for my parking!

ME: Sir, you been here for over thirty minutes, you used our service, so no, you cannot have a refund.

AUTOMOBILE TAX ADVISOR: What a rip off! I am never bringing clients here again!

ME: Good idea.

Before that day, I didn't think there could be a worse place to have your taxes done than at the kiosk in Wal-Mart behind the checkout stands. The Wal-Mart tax kiosk is in plain sight for everyone walking in or out of the store, not to mention everyone can hear your conversation with the tax preparer. But, like everything else in that parking lot, a new low was always within reach. Only the parking lot could make a Wal-Mart kiosk seem appealing.

BOGO Bliss

Sometimes, it is the little things that excite people. On the Friday before Memorial Day Weekend, a man headed out of court and back to his car stopped by to offer me some life changing information.

BOGO BENNY: Hey, do you shop over at Publix?

ME: Every so often.

BOGO BENNY: You need to be there, TODAY!

ME: I do?

BOGO BENNY: Yes! They got them buy one get one free watermelons!

ME: I did not know that.

BOGO BENNY: Them bitches BOGO'd watermelons! Got mine yesterday, the big ass ones! I'mma go back for two more today! Shit's going on all weekend up there!

ME: Sounds great, sir.

BOGO BENNY: *With great concern.* You better hurry before they're gone! Them melons be flyin the fuck outta there! Really, where you gonna get free fuckin' melons this time of year? Tis the season for that shit! BBQ's and shit, everyone be eatin' melon!

ME: I just may call my boss and ask to leave early.

BOGO BENNY: Now you talkin! You know what's up! Go get yours before them bitches wipe the box clean!

ME: I appreciate it, sir.

BOGO BENNY: *Extending his hand for a shake.* Don't say I never told you nothing!

ME: *Shaking Benny's hand.* I'll never be able to say that ever again.

BOGO BENNY: You know what's good! Have a blessed day!

ME: You too, enjoy the melon!

BOGO BENNY: Oh, you bet I will, I'm gettin' into that shit soon as I get home! Refreshing as fuck!

Despite Benny's strong recommendation, I never made it down to Publix that Memorial Day weekend. While the rest of my summer went well, the fact that I missed out on that BOGO watermelon haunted me well into late September.

Wichita Walk Off

Despite the half dozen "PAY AT BOOTH" signs throughout the parking lot, some people thought parking was free. For some reason, the word "public" had them assuming parking was free. It was a nonstop battle every day for me to explain otherwise. I'd keep an eye out all day for walk-offs. Most people I caught walking off without paying played dumb and said that they did not know they had to pay. Others simply were dumb.

ME: *Screaming out the window at a guy walking off without paying.* Sir! You have to pay for your parking!

The man continued to walk away until some of the other customers who heard me summoning him got involved and yelled at him to come to pay.

KANSAS KEN: What's the problem?

ME: Sir, you have to pay to park.

KANSAS KEN: Your sign says it is public parking!

ME: Public does not mean free, sir. And there are also a half dozen signs that say "Pay At Booth" one of which you drove past when you came in, another you walked past as you were walking away.

KANSAS KEN: Public means free!

ME: No sir, public means accessible to the general population.

KANSAS KEN: You are full of shit! Where I'm from public means free!

ME: Well, I'm not sure where you are from, but the school system there failed you.

KANSAS KEN: I'm from Wichita, not from a shithole town like this! So fuck you! I hate it here, having to pay for everything!

ME: Well sir, welcome to the big city. And guess what? It's not free here, you're not in Kansas anymore, so pay to park or click your heels three times and get the fuck out!

Kansas Ken stormed back to his car and drove away in search of the free parking that did not exist anywhere in town. If he only had a brain, he could park and be merry, if he only had a brain.

The Subpar Salutation

My standard greeting when someone came up to the payment window to pay for their parking was "Good morning (or afternoon) sir/ma'am, how are you today?" After the transaction was complete, I would say "Have a great day" or "Have a great rest of your day" if it was later in the day. I tried to mix it up a bit. Fridays included "Have a great weekend" or if it was a holiday weekend "Have a great holiday" or "Have a great holiday weekend." No matter what I said, I always tried to show thanks for the customers' business and leave them with a smile. But even my salutations had to be overanalyzed from time to time.

ME: Good Morning sir, how are you today?

ENTHUSIASTIC ERIC: Great, man! It's Friday!

ME: Been waiting for today since Sunday night.

ENTHUSIASTIC ERIC: Same here! I'm paying for spot 47.

ME: Ok great sir, that'll be five dollars, please.

ENTHUSIASTIC ERIC: Here you go.

ME: Thank you, sir. Here's your change and your ticket, have a great weekend!

ENTHUSIASTIC ERIC: You too, man! Enjoy!

ME: May I help the next person in line?

ME: Good morning, ma'am, how are you today?

PETTY PATTY: I'm ok, a little tired.

ME: I hear that! What space are you paying for today?

PETTY PATTY: Space 34, right over there.

ME: Ok great, that'll be five dollars.

PETTY PATTY: Do you have change of a fifty?

ME: Sure do.

PETTY PATTY: Here you go.

ME: Thanks so much, here is your change! Have a great day!

PETTY PATTY: Have a great day? What do you mean?

ME: I mean I hope your day goes well!

PETTY PATTY: Why did the guy before me get a "Have a great weekend" and I only got a "Have a great day."

ME: *Laughing, thinking she's joking.*

PETTY PATTY: I'm dead serious! What the fuck? You have a problem with me?

ME: You are being serious?

PETTY PATTY: Damn straight I am! How does he get wishes for a great weekend, and I only get a day? You should treat everyone the same!

ME: There was no bad intent ma'am, I just mix it up a bit so I'm not repeating the same thing all day.

PETTY PATTY: Seemed intentional to me!

ME: Well it wasn't. I'm sorry something so insignificant troubled you so much.

PETTY PATTY: I just want to be treated equally!

ME: Well, sorry you took offense.

PETTY PATTY: Fine, it is over, HAVE A GREAT WEEKEND!

ME: *Minimizing my initial salutation.* Have a great morning!

Petty Patty walked away while she mumbled something under her breath. Petty Patty's piss poor perspective on politeness would most likely prohibit her from having a prodigious day anyway. Patty was not the only one who took time out of her day to critique my salutations. I once said "Have a great day" to someone who replied "How the fuck am I going to have a great day, I'm at court!" so I replied with "Ok, then have a fucking terrible day!"

The Deductible Defendant

We live in an age where information is instantly available. Years ago, if you did not know who sang a particular song, you would call your friend and hum a few bars of the song hoping he or she would recognize it and give you the artist's name. Now you can Shazam, Google or find the artist a hundred different ways. Not feeling well? WebMD for your symptoms! Need a plumber? Head to Angie's List! Need legal forms? Head to LegalZoom! No matter what you need, it is available online. With all the information available out there with just a few clicks, I found it hard to believe that people came to a parking lot and asked me, the attendant, for all kinds of information and advice unrelated to parking. I've personally parked in parking lots all over, and it never dawned on me to ask the parking attendant to recommend a doctor, give relationship advice or rate a restaurant. I would park and go on my way. Not at the parking lot I managed.

ME: Hey, good morning sir, how's it going today?

DEDUCTIBLE DAN: Ok, I'm back again! Third day in a row!

ME: Well, nice to see you again.

A WHOLE LOT OF SHENANIGANS

DEDUCTIBLE DAN: You guys are taking all my money.

ME: Well, we thank you for your business!

DEDUCTIBLE DAN: Speaking of money, let me ask you something...

ME: *Thinking he's going to ask about a weekly parking rate. Ok, sure.*

DEDUCTIBLE DAN: Is all this tax deductible?

ME: Your parking?

DEDUCTIBLE DAN: That, and all this court stuff.

ME: Well, if you are here on business, I am sure you can deduct your parking expenses and your mileage.

DEDUCTIBLE DAN: What about the lawyer's fees?

ME: I'm not a tax accountant sir, but I would look into it if it is business related.

DEDUCTIBLE DAN: Well, I'm on trial for assault, so just wondering if I could deduct all this bullshit.

ME: Very doubtful you can deduct legal and other court related expenses for a non-work related matter, but again, I'm not a tax guy or a lawyer, so I'd consult with one.

DEDUCTIBLE DAN: But I am innocent! Why can't I deduct this if it's not my fault?

ME: Sir, I do not know the tax laws, I'd consult with someone in that field.

DEDUCTIBLE DAN: But you work here, right? Why wouldn't you know this stuff? I am sure people ask you stuff like this all the time. You should be trained in the laws!

ME: Sir, this is a privately owned business in the parking industry. Why would I have to learn tax laws?

DEDUCTIBLE DAN: Well you're near the courts! You deal with people going to court all day, it would be helpful!

ME: So, let me ask you something, should a parking attendant near a hospital be diagnosing sick people because he works near a hospital?

DEDUCTIBLE DAN: If it helps the customer, yes!

ME: Well, you mentioned you have a lawyer, why not consult with him about the tax stuff?

DEDUCTIBLE DAN: He's a criminal lawyer.

ME: I'm a parking attendant who is running a parking business, how am I more qualified than your lawyer?

DEDUCTIBLE DAN: You deal with all kinds of people, civil, criminal, etc., he just deals with criminals.

ME: Sir, we are getting nowhere here. I suggest you Google a tax accountant when you get home and give them a call for advice.

DEDUCTIBLE DAN: They'll probably charge me for a consultation.

ME: It'll be worth it. Asking tax advice from a parking attendant isn't the way to go.

DEDUCTIBLE DAN: Hey man, I gotta save where I can, this trial is costing me!

ME: I understand.

DEDUCTIBLE DAN: *Waving a twenty-dollar bill.* You sure you don't know the tax laws?

ME: No sir, call a tax accountant.

DEDUCTIBLE DAN: It was worth a shot.

The debate with Deductible Dan over tax advice finally concluded. It was then that I wished I had taken down the number of that Automobile Tax Advisor in the beat up SUV that

I had met a few weeks earlier. They would have been a match made in tax heaven. I'm certain that Deductible Dan is going to be in line for an IRS audit in the very near future.

Cold Case

Ever since September 11, 2001, the public has been told to be aware of their surroundings. "If you see something, say something" is the phrase we been told to follow. On one very cold winter morning, I pulled into the parking lot very early, as always. I noticed a large, silver suitcase, sitting all by itself in the corner of the parking lot, about fifty yards away from the county courthouse. It was not your regular run of the mill travel suitcase, it was one of those oversized, hard shelled suitcases. Something about it just did not look right, so I decided to call the local police precinct.

POLICE DISPATCH: City police, can I help you?

ME: Yes, I work across the street from the courthouses, I run a parking lot over there. I arrived this morning to find a hard silver suitcase just sitting in the corner of the lot. It looks suspicious.

POLICE DISPATCH: Ok, sir what is the address, we'll send a car over.

I gave the dispatcher my address and waited for the police car to arrive. About fifteen minutes later an office showed up, slurping on a large coffee.

COFFEE COP: Hey, what's going on? Something about a suitcase? Man, it is freezing out here today!

ME: Yes, sir, good morning. That suitcase sitting right over there looks pretty unusual.

COFFEE COP: Did you open it?

ME: Why would I open it?

COFFEE COP: *Laughing.* Is it ticking?

ME: I did not get that close.

COFFEE COP: Is it locked?

ME: I don't know officer; I did not touch or approach the suitcase.

COFFEE COP: Ok, let's go have a look.

ME: Ummmm, I'll stand here. You sure you don't want to call the bomb squad? I've seen roads and shopping centers closed off for a lot less than this. The courts are fifty yards away.

COFFEE COP: *Taking another big gulp of coffee.* Yeah, I guess, but why create a stir? I'll go open it.

The Coffee Cop walked over to the suitcase and gave it a couple of kicks.

COFFEE COP: Shit, whatever it is, it's heavy! I don't hear any ticking.

ME: You sure you want to open that?

COFFEE COP: *Popping the clips on the case.* Here goes!

The Coffee Cop opened the case and took a quick step back.

COFFEE COP: Holy Shit!

ME: What? Is it a bomb? Should I call someone else?

COFFEE COP: This is worth a whole heap of money!

ME: What is in there?

COFFEE COP: A whole bunch of cameras, lenses, and equipment! This is professional shit, worth thousands!

ME: Maybe it was stolen and dumped, you should take it with you.

COFFEE COP: Too much paperwork, you can hold onto it just in case the owner comes back for it.

ME: I don't think someone accidentally left this here, but we do have news reporters and networks filming in the parking lot every so often about a court case, so perhaps they left it. I'll put it inside my booth, but let me put gloves on first to carry it over, don't want my prints on it in case it is stolen stuff.

I walked over to my booth and put on a pair of latex surgical gloves that I kept in the booth for handling trash and other gross things regularly dumped in the lot. I then took the case and placed it inside the booth.

COFFEE COP: I guess wait a few days, then sell it on eBay!

ME: Don't think I am comfortable with that, but I'll keep it here for a while and let the owner of the lot know about it.

COFFEE COP: Ok, whatever you want to do. I'd sell it! Finders keepers! Stay warm! Have a good day!

ME: You too, thanks!

The Coffee Cop left me holding the bag. Literally, holding the bag. I tucked it away inside the booth and went on with my day. The next afternoon the Coffee Cop and a couple of other officers pulled into the lot and came up to the window.

COFFEE COP: You still have that equipment, or did you sell it already?

ME: It's right in here.

COFFEE COP: *Showing me a police report.* Turns out there was a house burglary in the area last Sunday night and this is one of many items that were stolen from the house.

ME: Glad I didn't touch the case!

COFFEE COP: Yeah, I probably should have worn gloves myself, hopefully we can still get prints off of it.

ME: Ok officer, come on in, I'll give you a pair of gloves and you can carry it out of here.

COFFEE COP: Do you have a plastic garbage bag? I want to place it in something to preserve any possible prints.

ME: That ship may have sailed already, but yes, I can give you a trash bag.

The Coffee Cop, with his gloves on, placed the case into a white kitchen trash bag and put it in the trunk of his police car.

COFFEE COP: Glad you didn't put it on eBay, or we'd be knocking on your door.

ME: I had no intention of selling it on eBay, but had I been stupid enough to do that, I would have sent the cops to you since that was your idea.

COFFEE COP: *Nervously laughing in front of two other officers.* Yeah, not the best advice, I guess. Ok, well no harm done! Thanks for everything!

ME: No problem, I am sure the owners will be glad to have them back!

After the Coffee Cop, suitcase incident, I did not feel quite as safe as I once did in that town. Think about it, a cop showed up to a suspicious package call, asked me if I opened it, joked about it ticking, kicked it, handled it without gloves, opened it, would not take it with him because it involved paperwork, told me to sell the contents on eBay, then showed up a day later with an "oops," it was part of a burglary and was stolen property and possibly evidence. Did I work in fuckin' Mayberry? I did subconsciously whistle the Andy Griffith theme song each time I saw an officer from that town from that point forward.

Overheard in the Lot

This collection of parking lot shenanigans would not be complete without some eloquent quotes from the people that made this book possible, the parkers. Standing in that window, day after day, I saw and heard it all. Here are some great overheard conversations from the now infamous parking lot.

Young guy on his cell phone leaving court: "I'm da motherfuckin' Teflon Don! I beat them charges like Rocky! Eye of the tiger bitch, eye of the motherfuckin' tiger! Adriaaaaaaaaaaaane!"

Twenty-something woman to her friend: "That Burger King sure tasted good going in last night, but you wouldn't believe the smell coming out in that toilet this morning! You wouldn't have wanted to be within five miles of that toilet after I shit it all out!"

Woman on her cell phone: "So, we finally had sex last night, but I think his dog was sniffing my ass when I was riding him."

Old woman crossing in the middle of a four lane road, against the light, forcing cars to come to a screeching halt while waving her cane in the air and screaming, "Just like Moses baby, just like motherfuckin' Moses!"

Lady to her friend after taking a huge handful of mints out of the bowl I had put out as a courtesy for customers: "You think they'd put out some of those fuckin' Reese's. What's with these raggedy ass mints?"

Man on his cell phone: "Yeah I am leaving court now. I'm going right home, not going to the office. I think I got food poisoning. Yeah, I got Chinese last night and it ran through me like Sherman ran through Atlanta."

Woman on cell phone: "Yeah I'm up here now gettin' them divorce papers. How he gonna fuck that wig wearin', fake bag carryin', no money making ho up in my bed? He's motherfuckin' finished!"

Old guy to his friend: "All this gay shit! Now they are even trying to tell kids that Bert and Ernie are homosexuals! Imagine two puppets fucking each other in the ass? It's gotten out of hand!"

Woman on cell phone: "No, she's not gift wrapping material, bitch is getting it in a gift bag! She's lucky I got her anything! Got no time to wrap for that bitch!"

Woman to her friend on the day after Halloween: "That cheap ass ho' gave out them fun size candies last night! Who be givin' out fun size? Her man probably got a fun size dick, that's where she be getting' fun size from!"

Guy to his girlfriend after she wrapped his head in fake bandages and handed him crutches before they headed into court: "Thanks bae, we gonna get motherfuckin' paid in there! Cha-motherfuckin'-ching!"

Young guy on his cell phone: "I didn't know she was such a ho! That bitch be cuckoo for my cocoa cock!"

Woman on her cell phone on the day before a winter storm: "Not a loaf of bread left! Yeah, I'm gonna try another store. You think these rednecks would be wiping out the applesauce aisle since they ain't got no teeth to chew all that bread!"

Guy on his cell phone: "That new BBQ place is great! Yeah, we went last night! So fuckin' big! The ribs were so big they reminded me of the Flintstones. Yeah, that big ass rib that tips over the car, that's how big this rack of ribs was!"

Guy on his cell phone leaving court: "Yeah my baby mama got more drama in that court than one of them Lifetime movies. All we needed was some tampon commercials up in that shit."

Woman on her cell phone: "You see that fat bitch in that purple dress on Facebook? She look like Grimace from them old McDonald's commercials! Oooh yeah, you right girl, like motherfuckin' Barney!"

Guy to his friend: "You think the guy in there (*referring to me*) will let me change my pants in his booth?"
Other guy: "Bro, that's the gayest thing you've ever said."
Guy: "Yeah, that was pretty gay."

Guy on his cell phone: "It's hotter out here than two rats fucking in a wool sock on the fourth of July!"

Woman on her cell phone: "Gloria has been staying with us. Yeah, ok, I guess. Oh, did I tell you she took a shit and didn't flush? I know, it was so big it looked like the Titanic when it was sinking."

Guy talking to his friend: "Can't believe Michael Jackson died today."
Friend: "Michael Jackson be dead for years already bro! Prince died today!"
Guy: "Ain't they the same? I thought Prince was like his alter-ego and shit."

Woman on cell phone: "Honey, you'll never get anywhere in life if you procrastinate! Listen, I gotta run, I'm like an hour late!"

Guy on his cell phone: "No more probation! I can smoke weed again! I'm done! Like Daffy Duck used to say, that's all folks! Oh, it was Bugs Bunny? Same shit!

And that truly is all, folks!

About the Author

Charlie A. McMahon was born and raised on Long Island in New York. He and his wife moved to the Atlanta Metro area shortly after his 40th birthday. Charlie lives in Smyrna, Georgia with his wife, three dogs and cat. This is his first book. He hosts the weekly podcast A Bunch of Malarkey. This book, like his podcast, was inspired by his knack for finding humor in everyday experiences.

27091558R00134

Made in the USA
Columbia, SC
26 September 2018